Estee Kafra's

Cooking with
COLOR

dinner

Design and Layout: RB CREATIVE
www.rbcreativedesign.com

Photographs and Food Styling: ST Studio
www.ststudio.ca

Edited by: Norene Gilletz, kosher cookbook author
www.gourmania.com

Distributed by: Israel Book Shop
501 Prospect Street #97, Lakewood, NJ 08701
Telephone: 732-901-3009   Fax: 732-901-4012
www.israelbookshoppublications.com

Printed in China

See My creations, how beautiful and praiseworthy they are;
and everything that I created I created for you.

Ecclesiastes, Rabbah 7:13

ACKNOWLEDGEMENTS

A book is only a success with a strong team behind it. I want to thank the following individuals who selflessly contributed their time and talents:

The staff at Binah Magazine – Mrs. B. Lichtenstein, Mrs. R. Roth, Pam Sherr, Rochel Bashi Binik, Toby Morgenstern and Mr. Glick for their expertise, vision and endless patience. You are a great team.

Mimi Rosenberg, for once again being the "good messenger."

Rivki Bakst of RB Creative. Rivki, you did it again! Your artistic flair is obvious throughout both books. It is a pleasure working with you.

Norene Gilletz – Your experience and attention to detail helped take this project to a whole new level. Not only are you a super talent, you're also fun to worth with. Thanks for everything.

My Husband and children – Thank you for your patience, understanding and support. You are the greatest group of taste-testers ever.

To my parents, in-laws, grandparents and siblings – Thank you for always being there with a listening ear and a lending hand. Thanks Sari for holding the reflector with a smile.

To a great group of friends and family whose personal interest and great ideas are apparent throughout the book. Thank you to Faigy Grossman, Dassi Slater, Mrs. Leah Grosz, Mrs. Chumie Steinmetz, Mrs. Noami Friedman, Leah Frankel, Dina Gunsburg, Deborah Jacobs, the "lunch chevra" and the "cooking club."

Reva Kaiser Wein – Thanks for the professional and excellent job you did with the text.

A special thank you to my Aunt Lily who inspired me to preserve the fruits of summer, and gave me step by step instructions and guidance.

Israel Bookshop – Once again it is a pleasure doing business with you.

Behind the scenes helpers – Puerita Miranda, Celeste Porras, Clair Pereira and Jayne Jones.

Thank you to the wonderful community of Toronto for your feedback and enthusiasm, I really appreciate it.

contents

DEAR READER,

A friend of mine recently asked what it was that prompted me to write another cook book only one year after my first book, "Spice it Right!" was published. As I contemplated her question, I realized that it was actually you, dear readers, who were the impetus. The overwhelmingly enthusiastic responses that I received from all corners of the world were really what pushed me to start the long and challenging, but fun process of writing another book. Compiled here are some really terrific recipes, some of which have been previously printed in Binah Magazine and others which were developed, collected and perfected especially for you.

I have chosen the earth's bounty as the theme for this book because it inspires me. When I shop for fruits and vegetables and I am surrounded by the vibrant array of colors, shapes and, of course, distinct tastes, I feel challenged to experiment and try new ways to use the wonderful variety that G-d created. I have included a step-by-step guideline for those interested in preserving your delicious creations. Give it a try. Once you have mastered it there is no turning back.

There are a few things I always keep in mind when working with a recipe. I try to ensure it is relatively simple. Life seems to get busier and busier, with less time to spend in the kitchen on recipes with too many steps. Also, the less utensils and bowls that need to be washed afterwards, the better. I also try to stay true to the flavor of the produce I am cooking. Grilling, blanching, steaming and roasting are all excellent ways to maintain authentic flavors.

I hope you enjoy both the dinner and dessert books as much as I do and that you, too, are inspired to try new things and come to love the adventure of Cooking with Color!

Estee

Vegetables

What I love most about vegetables is that they are so versatile! They seem to find their way into so much of our regular cooking, whether it's tossing some cabbage and zucchini into a soup, throwing together cucumbers and tomatoes for a quick chef's salad, or simply sautéing onions for a chicken or meat dish. Veggies are great raw, cooked, steamed, sautéed or even grilled! Alone, or as an accompaniment, they're satisfying and delicious. Even young children can be easily coaxed into snacking on slivered carrot sticks or those sweet, bite-sized grape tomatoes. What's also pretty amazing about vegetables is the incredible variety to which we have access, with the added bonus that they are all so tasty and nutritious.

GROUPS

Vegetables are generally organized into the following ten groups, to which I've added some well-known examples:

ROOT Carrots, turnips, parsnips, celeriac, radishes

TUBERS Potatoes, sweet potatoes, jerusalem artichokes, jicimas, casava, yams

BULBS Onions (various varieties), shallots, leeks, chives, garlic

LEAVES Cabbage, spinach, lettuce (all different types), watercress, bok choy

FLOWER HEADS Cauliflower, broccoli, globe artichoke

STEMS Celery, fennel, asparagus

PEAS + LEGUMES Sugar snap peas, string beans, garden peas

FUNGI Mushrooms

VEGETABLE FRUIT Tomatoes, avocado, eggplants, cucumbers, zucchini or courgette, squash, corn, chili peppers, peppers, winter squash

HEALTH BENEFITS

The US Department of Health recommends that we eat three to five servings of vegetables each day. When you toss up a fresh salad with just one cup of raw, leafy greens (like lettuce) and ½ cup of other vegetables – cooked or raw (think peppers, cucumbers, mushrooms) – you already have two servings of healthy veggies on your plate. Enjoy this with ¾ cup of your favorite vegetable juice (like carrot, tomato or a blend), and you've already met the minimum amount of suggested servings in one delicious, nutritious snack!

So first our mothers and now the government want us to eat our vegetables. Why is everyone so into this? Because they really are so incredibly good for us! Vegetables are loaded with antioxidants that help heal and protect the body from various diseases and most may also prevent cancer. We all appreciate that vegetables come in a rainbow of colors that are so helpful in creating a bright, eye-catching salad, or dressing up a dish. But did you know that you can tell a lot about a vegetable's (or fruit's) health benefits simply by its color?

(The following benefits are all in addition to the healing, protective and cancer-preventative abilities of vegetables and fruit in general.)

Red produce, such as tomatoes, rhubarb and red peppers promote heart and urinary tract health and improve memory function.

The color orange is a must in your daily diet, since produce this color – such as sweet potatoes and carrots – contain vitamin C, folate and beta-carotene, a natural antioxidant that may boost the immune system. And we just thought carrots were good for your eyesight!

Loaded with minerals, fiber and essential vitamins like folate, green vegetables such as spinach, kale and broccoli also have antioxidants that promote eye health, boost the immune system and help build strong bones and teeth.

So beautiful and serene-looking, blue and purple fruits and vegetables like eggplant, grapes and blueberries are full of antioxidants that promote healthy aging, urinary tract health and memory function. We've all heard about the famous health benefits of the little blueberry!

And last, but not least, let's not forget about white, a color that appears in onions, garlic, chives, leeks, cucumbers and cauliflowers. The antioxidants in these basic vegetables help us maintain a healthy cholesterol level, promote a healthy heart and boost the immune system.

PREPARATION

Now that we can appreciate the nutritious boost we're giving ourselves and those we're feeding when we serve vegetables, here are a few tips to help you along in some of the many methods of vegetable preparation.

Steaming is a fast and convenient way to cook vegetables. It is also probably the best method to bring out a vegetable's deepest flavor. Sometimes I just add a simple sauce or a quick sprinkle of kosher or sea salt to give steamed vegetables that extra zing, but that's really all they need. Steamed vegetables also maintain many of their natural vitamins and nutrients, making this method a preferred, healthy way of cooking.

To steam, cut your vegetables in similar sized pieces to promote uniform cooking throughout. Fill a pot with 1 to 2 inches of water and add a steamer insert. Over high heat, bring the water to a boil. Put the vegetables in the steamer, trying not to overlap them too much, and sprinkle them with kosher salt. Cover the pot tightly and steam just until tender. Of course, different vegetables will vary in their cooking times. Green beans or broccoli may take about four minutes, while baby potatoes may take as long as 15 minutes. Don't forget to ensure that there is enough water in the pot with those vegetables that require longer cooking times.

Blanching is a simple technique for keeping vegetables crisp and tender. By cooking vegetables briefly and then dunking them into an ice bath to stop the cooking, this process helps preserve the ideal texture, color and flavor of the vegetable.

To blanch, bring a pot of salty water to a rapid boil over high heat. Prepare a bowl filled with ice water. Cook the vegetables for a few minutes, which will take them just past their raw state, but preserves their crunchiness. In this short time, the color of most veggies will brighten. Taste one, and if it's ready, remove the rest from the pot and place them in the ice water to immediately stop the cooking process.

When I blanch small vegetables such as corn kernels or peas, I like to contain them in a colander, which makes it easy to first dip the vegetables into the boiling water and then the ice water. This is especially good to do when you'll be cooking other vegetables as well, which can be cooked in the same water afterwards.

Freezing fresh vegetables will give you bags of yummy produce at your fingertips. Frozen vegetables are great for soups, casseroles and just about any cooked dish. To freeze veggies, first blanch them. After one minute in the ice water, drain and dry the vegetables very well with paper towels. Lay them out on a lined cookie sheet, which should be placed in the freezer for 2 to 3 hours until frozen solid. Once frozen, transfer the vegetables into freezer bags, making them as airtight as possible. Frozen vegetables can be stored (frozen, of course) for up to three months. I like to double bag them to prevent the vegetables from picking up odors in the freezer.

Caramelizing is most often used in reference to onions, though many other vegetables can be caramelized as well. Caramelized onions form the base of many delicious recipes, especially onion soups. When caramelizing a vegetable, it cooks over a low flame for a long time so that the water in the vegetable evaporates. At a certain temperature, the sugars in the vegetable begin to break down and that causes the vegetable to brown. When caramelizing, use a heavy, non-stick pan to prevent the vegetables from sticking, and thus reduce the risk of burning. Vegetables with low water and high sugar content are the best candidates for caramelizing. Most members of the onion family, including leeks, and vegetables such as carrots, fennel and peppers are delicious when cooked using this method. Sometimes a recipe calls for sugar to be added to enhance the process.

These symbols indicate weather the recipe is made with Meat, Dairy or Pareve (contain no meat or dairy) ingredients.

GENERAL COOKING TERMS

CHOP To cut food into small pieces.

CORE The hard, central part of an apple, pear, etc., that contains the seeds; to remove the core of the fruit.

CUBE To cut solid food into cubes about ½ inch or more in size.

DICE To make small cubes ⅛ to ¼ inch in size.

GRATE To rub food (often cheese, vegetables and the rinds of citrus fruits) against an instrument that shreds it.

GRIND To reduce a food to very small pieces in a grinder, blender or food processor.

JULIENNE To cut fruits, vegetables or meat into match-like strips.

MINCE To cut or chop food into very fine pieces.

PURÉE To put food through a sieve, blender or processor to produce a thick pulp or paste.

SAUTÉ To brown or cook in a small amount of fat.

SCORE To make shallow slits into the food, usually in a rectangular or diamond pattern.

SHRED To cut into long thin strips with a knife or shredder.

SIMMER To cook in liquid just below the boiling point over a low heat.

STEAM To cook in a covered container over boiling water.

STIR FRY To cook with a small amount of fat in a frying pan or wok over high heat, stirring constantly.

SWEAT To cook gently – usually in butter, a bit of oil or the food's own juices – in order to soften but not brown the food.

VEGETABLE	STORAGE LOCATION	TIME
Artichokes	room temperature	several weeks
Asparagus	in the fridge, standing upright in 1-inch of water	7 to 10 days
Beans	keep refrigerated	1 to 2 weeks
Beets	keep refrigerated	up to 3 weeks
Broccoli	keep refrigerated	1 week
Cabbage	crisper	several weeks
Carrots	in plastic bag in the fridge	up to four weeks
Cauliflower	keep refrigerated	up to a week
Celery	keep refrigerated	up to 10 days
Cucumbers	keep refrigerated	7 to 10 days
Eggplants	keep refrigerated	7 to 10 days
Endives	crisper	up to 2 weeks
Garlic	hang in a mesh bag in a dry, airy spot (never let the bulbs get wet)	several weeks
Ginger	dry, cool place	several weeks
Kohlrabi	keep refrigerated	7 to 10 days
Leeks	keep refrigerated	7 to 10 days
Lettuce	in the refrigerator's crisper after being washed and spun in a salad spinner	7 to 10 days
Mushrooms	in a paper bag in the fridge	5 to 7 days
Onions	store separately from other vegetables in a cool, dry place in a mesh bag or basket to allow for air circulation	several months
Parsnips	keep refrigerated	2 to 3 weeks
Peas	keep refrigerated	few days
Potatoes	dry, cool, dark location with good air circulation	few weeks
Pumpkin	cool, airy location	several months
Radishes	crisper	7 to 10 days
Shallots	cold, dry location	several months
Spinach	keep refrigerated	up to a week
Sweet Corn	keep refrigerated	as soon as possible
Sweet potatoes	dry location (do not refrigerate)	up to 4 months
Tomatoes	keep refrigerated (but they will tend to lose their flavor there)	2 to 4 weeks
	to quicken the ripening process and maximize their flavor, leave on counter	several days
Turnips	in or out of the fridge	several weeks
White radishes	keep refrigerated	several weeks
Zucchini	keep refrigerated	up to a week

ARTICHOKE

BROCCOLI

CAULIFLOWER

breads

WALNUT BREAD

This recipe is sort of a hybrid: it's half bread and half cake, and is a spin on a traditional Hungarian walnut babke. Serve it toasted with the spiced butter for a real treat. I have it here in a brioche pan, although I might even prefer it done jelly-roll style and baked in a loaf pan – both ways are delicious!

2 Tbsp active dry yeast

½ cup + 2 Tbsp sugar

2 cups warm water (105° to 155° F)

2 eggs

2 egg yolks

½ cup canola oil

6 cups all-purpose flour

2 tsp kosher salt

Oil for brushing

Filling:

3 cups finely chopped walnuts

1 cup sugar

1 tsp ground cinnamon, optional

Glaze and Topping:

1 egg yolk

1 Tbsp honey

Additional chopped walnuts for sprinkling

1 Place yeast, sugar, and warm water into the bowl of a mixer fitted with a dough hook. Let stand 5 minutes until bubbly. Add remaining ingredients, leaving salt for last. Let mix for 5 to 7 minutes on medium-high speed. The dough should be a wet dough; if necessary, add 1 to 2 more tablespoons flour to pull it together. Cover and let rise for 1 hour at room temperature until double in size.

2 Mix chopped walnuts, sugar and cinnamon together in a bowl. Divide dough into 2 or 3 pieces and roll thin. Brush with oil and sprinkle generously with walnut sugar mixture. Roll up tightly and place in a well-greased high round pan or a loaf pan. Repeat with remaining dough and filling. Cover and let rise for 1 hour more.

3 Preheat oven to 350°F. Mix egg yolk with honey. Brush dough with egg wash and sprinkle with additional chopped walnuts. Let bake for 40 minutes.

SPICED BUTTER Soften 3 Tbsp unsalted whipped butter to room temperature. Mix in 1 tsp cinnamon, a pinch of ground cloves and a pinch of ground nutmeg. Refrigerate until needed.

Yield: 3 medium loaves or 2 large loaves

WHOLE WHEAT ONION ROLLS

There's nothing like fresh onion rolls, straight from the oven. Try them with dill butter – they are really good!

2¼ cups warm water (105° to 115°F)

1 Tbsp sugar

2½ Tbsp dry instant yeast

2 eggs

4 Tbsp honey

½ cup canola oil

2½ cups white bread flour

4 cups whole wheat flour

2½ tsp kosher salt

Filling:

1 or 2 large Vidalia onions, diced

4 Tbsp extra-virgin olive oil

2 Tbsp poppy seeds, plus more for sprinkling

Egg Wash:

1 egg yolk

1 Tbsp water

1 Combine warm water, sugar, and yeast in the bowl of an electric mixer fitted with a dough hook. Let stand 5 minutes, until bubbly. Add remaining ingredients, leaving the salt for last. Mix for 5 minutes on medium-high speed. Place dough in a greased bowl, turning it over so that the entire surface of the dough is greased. Cover and let rise for about 1 hour, until double in size.

2 Meanwhile, heat olive oil in a large pan. Sauté onions on medium heat until transparent and just beginning to brown. Set aside and cool.

3 Lightly grease 12 compartments of a muffin pan and set aside. Preheat oven to 350°F.

4 Cut dough into 12 even pieces and roll each piece into a circle. Place a tablespoon of onions into the center of each circle. Sprinkle with poppy seeds and close dough by joining the outer edges together and pinching them closed, almost creating a sack for the onions. Turn upside down and place seam-side down into lightly greased muffin pans. (Alternatively, you can create rolls by rolling out each piece into a rope between your palms and then flattening the rope with a rolling pin. Spoon some onions along the whole length of the dough and roll it up like a cinnamon bun. Place in lightly greased muffin pans.) Cover and let rise 45 to 60 minutes.

5 Brush with egg wash and sprinkle additional poppy seeds or fried onions, if desired. Bake for 25 to 30 minutes. Remove from muffin pan and cool on wire rack.

DILL BUTTER Combine 1 tsp dry dill, 2 Tbsp softened whipped butter and ½ tsp salt (if butter is unsalted) in a bowl and mix with the back of a spoon.

Yield: 12 Rolls

NEW YORK BAGELS

When my taste testers tried these bagels they told me that these tasted like authentic New York bagels: crispy on the outside and chewy on the inside.

1½ cups warm water (105° to 115°F)

2 Tbsp sugar

1 Tbsp dry instant yeast

4 cups + 2 Tbsp bread flour

1 Tbsp salt

8 to 10 cups water

1 Tbsp sugar

2 tsp salt

Sesame seeds, poppy seeds, and kosher salt (optional)

1 Place warm water, sugar and yeast into a large bowl and let stand 5 minutes, until bubbly. Add flour and salt and mix for about 2 minutes until a stiff dough forms (you may need to add 2 more tablespoons of water). Place dough in a greased bowl, turning it over so that the entire surface of the dough is greased. Cover dough and let rise in a warm place for 45 minutes to 1 hour (dough will not double in size).

2 Punch dough down and cut into 10 or 12 even pieces. Form each piece into a smooth ball. Poke a finger through the center and twirl the ball of dough around your finger to enlarge the hole. (When preparing the dough in advance, you can place the formed dough onto a greased baking sheet, cover tightly, and refrigerate overnight.)

3 Heat a large pot of water (about 8 to 10 cups) and bring to a boil. Add sugar and salt. Preheat oven to 425°F.

4 Drop the bagels in batches of 3 or 4 into the boiling water (do not overcrowd) and cook on each side for about 1½ minutes. Remove from pot and place on a towel to absorb excess moisture.

5 Place bagels on a greased cookie sheet and sprinkle with sesame or poppy seeds and kosher salt. Bake for 25 to 28 minutes.

Yield: 10 to 12 Bagels

PITA

Whether filled with schnitzel and fries, schwarma or chocolate spread, pitas are not only popular but are a mainstay of the Israeli diet. Over the last few decades, the pita's popularity has spread worldwide.

1 Tbsp active dry yeast

1 tsp sugar

1¾ cups warm water (105° to 115°F)

2 tsp salt

2½ Tbsp extra-virgin olive oil

4½ cups flour

1 Place yeast, sugar, and hot water into the bowl of an electric mixer fitted with a dough hook. Let stand 5 minutes, until bubbly. Add remaining ingredients and mix for a full 5 minutes. Transfer dough to a greased bowl. Cover with a towel, turning it over so that the entire surface of the dough is greased. Let rise 30 to 45 minutes.

2 Cut dough into 10 even pieces for large pitas, or 16 to 20 smaller pieces for mini pitas. Don't stretch or handle dough too much. Cover with a damp towel for 10 minutes.

3 Preheat oven to 500°F.

4 Roll each piece of dough gently to create a disc about 1 inch thick and place on a greased cookie sheet. Bake for about 5 minutes or until slightly puffed. Remove from oven and cover with a towel to keep soft. Once cooled, seal in a plastic bag. Serve within 24 hours.

NOTE For whole wheat pitas, replace 2½ cups of white flour with whole wheat flour.

Yield: 10 large or 15 to 20 small Pitas

CINNAMON CHALLAH CAKE

When the challah comes out of the oven on Friday afternoon, the house smells heavenly. Here is a great, easy way to use the challah dough so that everyone can share a pre-Shabbos treat that will be savored by all. I have personally used this recipe with much success at brunches and barbeques as well.

1 to 2 lbs challah dough

1 cup sugar

2 Tbsp ground cinnamon

Small bowl of room-temperature water

Raisins (optional)

1   Spray a Bundt pan with non-stick spray. (A springform or disposable pan can be used instead.)

2   Mix sugar and cinnamon in a bowl. Prepare a second bowl with about 2 cups of room temperature water.

3   Cut the dough into walnut-sized pieces, and roll between your hands to make them round. Dip the balls into the water and then roll in the cinnamon-sugar mixture. Place balls into the Bundt pan, just placing them loosely on top of each other until the pan is level at the top. (I like to throw in some raisins as well while I am filling the pan.) Cover and let rise for 1 hour.

4   Bake at 350°F for about 50 minutes.

NOTE   Use the recipe for Whole Wheat Challah on page 25, substituting whole wheat flour for bread flour.

Store-bought challah dough works very well too.

Yield: 1 challah with 10 servings

MY WHOLE WHEAT CHALLAH RECIPE

More than two and a half years ago, when I started writing for Binah Magazine, I put my challah dough recipe into one of the first issues. Since then, I have tweaked it and also played around with white whole wheat and regular whole wheat flour. You can use a larger percentage of whole wheat to white flour as long as it is 5 lbs in total.

4 Tbsp active dry yeast (or 4 oz. fresh yeast)

1¼ cups sugar

3 cups warm water (105° to 115°F)

2 cups additional water

3 eggs

1¼ cups canola oil

2½ lbs white bread flour

2½ lbs whole wheat flour

¼ cup kosher salt

Egg Wash:

1 egg yolk

1 Tbsp water

1 Place yeast, sugar and 3 cups water into the bowl of a mixer fitted with a dough hook. Let sit 8 to 10 minutes, until bubbly.

2 Add remaining ingredients, alternating wet and dry, with the kosher salt going last. Leave mixer on high speed for a full 10 minutes!

3 Place a bit of flour into a large food-safe platic bag or container, hold the top closed, and shake it up — flour will coat the inside of the bag. Place dough into the bag and knot at the top, leaving ample growing room. Let the dough rise about half an hour. (See Note.)

4 Separate challah, make a brachah, and divide dough into 5 or 6 parts. Braid challahs.

5 Let rise another 45 minutes to 1 hour. Brush with egg wash. Bake at 350°F for 45 to 50 minutes, until golden brown. (When you tap the loaves, they should sound hollow.)

NOTE As soon as you can handle the heat, remove challahs from pans and place sideways on a paper towel or towel, if you do not have a cooling rack.

Never use garbage bags for rising the dough as they may have been treated with insecticides.

VARIATION I sometimes substitute the 5 lbs of flour for 5 lbs whole wheat flour

Yield: Recipe makes 5 challahs, 10 servings each

WHOLE WHEAT PRETZEL NUGGETS

These are so addictive. I know because I make them, then I make them again… and again… and again!

1 envelope instant dry yeast (2¼ tsp)

2 Tbsp honey

1¾ cups apple juice (at room temperature)

2¼ cups whole wheat flour

2½ cups all-purpose flour

2½ Tbsp extra-virgin olive oil

2 tsp kosher salt (plus more for sprinkling)

Egg Wash:

1 beaten egg plus 1 tsp water

1 Preheat oven to 425°F. Lightly grease a baking sheet with oil.

2 Combine yeast, honey and apple juice in the bowl of an electric mixer fitted with a dough hook. Let stand a few minutes until mixture begins to foam. Add remaining ingredients, adding the salt last. Mix on medium speed for 3 to 4 minutes, until dough is smooth and well kneaded.

3 Cut dough into 10 equal pieces and roll each piece into a long rope about 1 inch thick, flouring your hands for easier handling. Cut each rope into 2-inch pieces; place pieces about 1-inch apart on prepared baking sheet.

4 Brush with egg wash and sprinkle with kosher salt.

5 Bake for about 18 minutes, until well browned. Let cool at least 5 minutes (if you can restrain yourself!) Dip into honey mustard for a great combination.

NOTE The dough may require up to ¼ cup additional apple juice to bring it together. It is meant to have a firmer consistency.

Yield: approximately 36 nuggets

FINGERLING

RUSSET

PURPLE
POTATO

RED
POTATO

YUKON
GOLD

SWEET
POTATO

JICAMA

YAM

breads

soup

salads

fish

meat + poultry

sides

dairy dishes

RED PEPPER CARROT SOUP

This colorful soup is a tasty way to have a serving of vegetables without a lot of fat. The orange juice and orange rind add a nice flavor, but the soup is delicious without it as well. You know your customers — act accordingly!

1 medium red pepper

1 ½ lbs carrots, sliced

1 medium onion, chopped

3 Tbsp uncooked long-grain rice

2 Tbsp oil

4 cups chicken soup

2 cups water

⅓ cup orange juice (optional)

2 tsp grated orange peel (optional)

2 tsp kosher salt

½ tsp freshly ground black pepper

1 Preheat oven to broil. Place whole red pepper in a foil pan. Broil it 4 inches from the heat until skin is blistered, about 6 minutes. Rotate until all sides are blistered and blackened. Immediately place pepper in a bowl; cover and let stand for 15 to 20 minutes. Peel and discard charred skin. Remove stem and seeds; set pepper aside.

2 In a large saucepan, cook the carrots, onion and rice in oil until onion is tender. Stir in the chicken soup, water, orange juice, orange peel (if using), salt, and pepper. Bring to a boil. Reduce heat; cover and simmer for 20 to 25 minutes or until carrots and rice are tender. Remove from heat and cool for 10 minutes.

3 In a blender, purée carrot mixture and roasted pepper in small batches. Return to the pan and heat through. Or, use an immersion blender in the saucepan and purée until smooth.

NOTE For a dairy version, you can substitute butter for the oil and water or vegetable broth for the chicken soup.

If you don't have time to roast the peppers, jarred red peppers (not the hot and spicy ones) can be substituted.

Yield: 8 to 10 servings

CAULIFLOWER SOUP

WITH CANDIED PINE NUTS

Even those who aren't cauliflower fans will enjoy this thick, creamy soup, perfect for any meal. The garnish really adds a nice flavor and can be made up to two weeks in advance, so double the recipe and have some on hand.

2 Tbsp olive oil

3 leeks (white parts only), chopped

1 zucchini, peeled and chopped

1 medium potato, peeled and chopped

2 lbs frozen cauliflower

1 Tbsp kosher salt

1 tsp white pepper

Water to cover (about 3 to 4 cups)

Candied Pine Nuts:

¼ cup sugar

½ cup pine nuts

1 In a large pot, heat olive oil. Add leeks, zucchini, and potato and let cook on low heat, stirring occasionally until just softened — about 5 to 10 minutes.

2 Add cauliflower, salt, and pepper. Add enough water to just cover the vegetables, and cook for about half an hour or until vegetables are very soft. Stir occasionally. Remove from heat and cool slightly.

3 Using an immersion blender, purée all the vegetables to a smooth consistency.

4 For candied pine nuts, place sugar and pine nuts in a heavy non-stick skillet or frying pan, over low heat, until sugar begins to melt.

5 As sugar is melting, keep stirring until the sugar is liquid enough to coat the nuts, but not too dark in color. Remove from heat and spread onto parchment paper. Let cool.

Yield: 5 servings

SPLIT PEA SOUP

Not only are split peas healthy for you, they are filling and satisfying. Served with crusty bread, this recipe can be a full meal.

1 lb green split peas, (2 to 2¼ cups)

1 Tbsp oil

1 clove garlic, minced

2 onions, chopped

2 large carrots, thinly sliced

2 stalks celery, thinly sliced

2 large pieces flanken (with bones)

6 cups chicken soup

4 cups water

2 Tbsp kosher salt

Black pepper to taste

1 Soak peas in triple the amount of cold water for 1 hour.

2 Heat 1 tablespoon oil in a large (10-quart) pot. Add garlic, onions, carrots, celery, and meat, and let sauté until soft, about 10 minutes. Drain split peas and add to pot along with liquids, salt, and pepper.

3 Bring to boil. Reduce heat, cover and simmer for a minimum of 1 hour, and a maximum of 2 hours. Stir occasionally.

4 Remove meat from pot and cut into bite-size chunks. Discard bones and fat. Add meat back into soup. Adjust seasonings to taste and enjoy!

Yield: 12 servings

CREAMY ASPARAGUS SOUP

WITH PARMESAN CROUTONS

This soup can be served both warm and chilled. Serve with store-bought croutons to follow the recipe below for a delicious, home-made option.

3 Tbsp butter

1 large onion, chopped

2 lbs fresh or frozen asparagus

1 ½ Tbsp flour

1 Tbsp lemon juice

Lowfat milk to cover (about 3 to 4 cups)

½ cup heavy cream

Garnish with chopped chives

Parmesan Croutons:

10 to 12 slices round melba toast (approximately)

Olive oil

½ cup grated Parmesan cheese

1 In a large pot on medium-low heat, melt butter and add onion. Sauté until transparent (not brown) and then add asparagus. Let cook until soft, stirring occasionally (about 5 minutes).

2 Add flour and lemon juice and mix. Slowly stir in enough milk to fully cover the asparagus. Add salt and pepper, cover and let simmer for about 20 minutes, stirring occasionally. cool slightly.

3 Blend until smooth using an immersion blender. (You might want to pour the soup through a sieve to catch any larger pieces, but don't find it necessary.)

4 Add heavy cream, and adjust seasonings. Garnish with chives and croutons and serve.

5 For the croutons, preheat toaster oven to 450°F.

6 Brush melba toasts with olive oil.

7 Place about half a teaspoon of Parmesan cheese onto each piece of melba toast and bake for about 3 to 4 minutes. Serve on top of soup.

NOTE If reheating, you may want to add about half a cup of water to thin slightly.

I always recommend using fresh vegetables as opposed to the frozen version. In order to clean asparagus properly one must remove the tops and the small "triangles" from along the stem. I find it easier to just peel the whole stalk, and then cut off the tops and a bit from the bottom.

Yield: 10 servings

ORIENTAL-STYLE CHICKEN SOUP

8 to 10 cups chicken soup or broth

½ cup enoki mushrooms (approximately)

½ cup carrots, julienned

½ cup chopped scallions

½ cup snow peas, sliced diagonally

8 to 10 store-bought beef kreplach or 8 to 10 matzah balls

1 Bring chicken soup to a boil. Add the vegetables and kreplach or matzah balls 5 minutes before you are ready to remove the soup from the heat.

Yield: 10 servings

CORN CHOWDER

The full flavor of freshly picked corn is captured in this thick, nutritious soup. Serve with crusty whole wheat baguettes.

5 ears of corn

1 Tbsp oil

1 Tbsp butter

1 large Spanish onion, chopped

2 cloves garlic, minced

1 large or 2 medium carrots, chopped

3 cups water

2 bay leaves

1 sprig fresh rosemary

3 cups low-fat milk

1 tsp kosher salt

½ tsp white pepper

1 Cut the kernels of corn off the cob. Set aside. Reserve 3 of the cobs.

2 Heat oil and butter in a large saucepan and sauté onions and garlic until soft. Add corn kernels and carrots and sauté for 10 minutes until they are beginning to soften. Add water, bay leaves and rosemary. Break 3 of the cobs in half and place into the water as well. Bring soup to a boil.

3 Lower heat and add milk. Season with salt and pepper and simmer on low heat for 35 to 45 minutes, until vegetables are soft. Stir occasionally.

4 Remove the corn cobs, bay leaves and rosemary and blend the soup with an immersion blender.

NOTE If the soup is too thick, thin with a bit more milk.

Yield: 6 servings

ROASTED TOMATO SOUP

WITH BASIL

This soup is full of healthy ingredients and bright, fresh flavor. It can be made in advance and gets even better after being chilled in the refrigerator. It will last up to 4 days if stored well.

6 to 8 medium tomatoes

Kosher salt and freshly ground black pepper

4 Tbsp olive oil, divided use

3 cloves garlic chopped

1 large onion, chopped

1 can (28 oz) crushed tomatoes

3 Tbsp tomato paste

1 heaping tsp dried thyme

½ tsp crushed red pepper flakes

2 Tbsp sugar

3 to 4 cups water

¼ to ½ cup chopped fresh basil leaves

1 Preheat oven to 400°F.

2 Slice tomatoes in half lengthwise and place cut-side up on a large rimmed baking sheet. Sprinkle with salt and pepper and drizzle with 3 Tbsp olive oil. Roast uncovered until tomatoes are nicely browned, 45 to 50 minutes, stirring occasionally.

3 Meanwhile, sauté garlic and onions in 1 Tbsp oil in a large pot until translucent.

4 Add roasted tomatoes, canned tomatoes, tomato paste, thyme, pepper flakes, sugar and water to pot and bring to a boil.

5 Cover and simmer on low heat for 10 to 15 minutes, stirring occasionally.

6 Remove from heat, stir in basil and let cool slightly. Purée using an immersion blender until smooth. (You can also pour the cooled soup into a blender and purée it.) Serve hot or cold.

SERVING SUGGESTION Slice a baguette into thin slices, brush lightly with olive oil and top with grated Cheddar cheese. Toast or broil until golden. Place a slice or two (depending on size) in each bowl of soup just before serving.

Yield: 6 to 8 servings

PEA SOUP

WITH HOMEMADE GARLIC CROUTONS

While split pea soup is a winter classic, there is no comparing the rich taste of a creamy pea soup made with fresh spring peas. (Frozen peas are a good alternative for great pea soup all year long). Serve with homemade garlic croutons that take only moments to prepare.

1 large Spanish onion, diced

2 leeks, chopped (white parts only)

2 Tbsp oil

1 cup fresh (or frozen) whole peas (shelled)

4 cups vegetable or chicken stock

Sea salt

Freshly ground black pepper, to taste

Croutons:

½ loaf whole wheat (or white) French bread

2 cloves garlic, minced

2 to 3 Tbsp olive oil

1 Sauté onions and leeks in oil in a medium-sized pot over medium-low heat until soft, about 5 minutes.

2 Add peas. Cover pot and let cook on low heat a few minutes longer.

3 Add vegetable or chicken stock and seasonings. Bring to a boil, reduce heat, cover and simmer for 20 minutes or until peas have softened. Stir occasionally.

4 Blend with an immersion blender. (You may want to pour soup through a strainer to remove any pieces.)

5 Fot the croutons, preheat oven or toaster to 450°F.

6 Slice bread into 1½-inch thick slices and then cut each slice into 4 cubes. Place in a bowl, add garlic and oil, and mix until coated.

7 Place croutons in a foil pan and bake until edges start to brown, about 5 to 6 minutes.

Yield: 8 servings

CABBAGE

ICEBERG

RADDICHIO

BOK
CHOY

SPINACH

ROMAINE

ARUGULA

breads

soup

salads

fish

meat + poultry

sides

AVOCADO GRAPE-FRUIT SALAD

This salad is fantastic! It is refreshing and crunchy, with a delicious balance of flavors. You can serve it as an appetizer, as pictured here, or toss everything together in a large bowl right before serving.

Salad:

1 large head romaine lettuce

2 pink grapefruits, peeled

2 avocados

½ cup toasted whole hazelnuts (filberts)

Dressing:

2 heaping Tbsp mayonnaise

¾ cup extra-virgin olive oil

2 cloves garlic, crushed

3 Tbsp honey

1 Tbsp + 1 tsp freshly squeezed lemon juice

2 Tbsp orange juice

1½ tsp kosher salt

1½ tsp freshly ground black pepper

1 To prepare the dressing, combine all ingredients in a deep bowl and use an immersion blender to blend until smooth. You can beat vigorously by hand as well.

2 For the salad, cut romaine lettuce very finely to create a shredded look: hold a bunch of stacked lettuce leaves and slice them thinly, crosswise.

3 Gently remove and discard the outer membrane of each piece of grapefruit.

4 Cut avocado into wedges and drop each wedge into a bowl filled with orange juice. (If preparing in advance, you can keep the avocado wedges immersed in orange juice in the refrigerator to keep them from browning.)

5 Crush the toasted hazelnuts by placing them in a bag and pounding with a meat tenderizer or rolling pin.

6 Combine lettuce, avocado wedges, and grapefruit segments on individual plates or in a serving bowl in desired fashion, and pour dressing over them. Sprinkle with toasted hazelnuts.

Yield: 10 servings

GREEN BEAN DELI SALAD

Here is a new twist on the typical green bean almondine side dish. If making in advance, add the slivered almonds as close to serving time as possible.

¾ lb green beans, trimmed

⅓ red onion, peeled and sliced very thinly

Kosher salt to taste

½ cup slivered almonds, toasted

3 to 4 slices pastrami

3 Tbsp oil

Dressing:

1 Tbsp mustard

1 Tbsp oil

2 Tbsp red wine vinegar

½ tsp black pepper

1 tsp kosher salt

1 Cook green beans in salted boiling water for about 5 minutes. Drain and rinse under ice cold water (to prevent them from becoming overcooked). Pat dry.

2 Meanwhile, cut pastrami into thin strips. Heat oil in pan on medium heat. Add pastrami and cook for about 3 to 4 minutes and then remove with a fork and let drain on a paper towel. Let cool.

3 Combine beans, pastrami and onion in a bowl and sprinkle with kosher salt. Mix all ingredients for dressing in a small bowl and pour over salad. Toss to coat.

4 Add almonds just before serving and toss again.

Yield: 6 servings

RICE NOODLES
WITH PEPPER MEDLEY

A beautiful medley of both color and taste. It can be served as a cold salad or a warm side dish. Personally, I like to pile the rice noodles onto a platter, creating a bird's-nest shape, and place the medley of peppers into the center.

1 red bell pepper

1 orange bell pepper

1 yellow bell pepper

2 stalks celery

1 small purple onion

2 Tbsp oil

½ tsp sugar

Kosher salt

Freshly ground black pepper to taste

1 (7 to 10 oz) pkg rice noodles

2 Tbsp additional oil

2 cloves garlic, minced

1 Finely dice the peppers, celery, and onion to about the same size. Heat oil in a skillet. Add vegetables and sauté on low heat until just beginning to soften. Add sugar, kosher salt, and black pepper. Remove from heat and set aside.

2 Meanwhile, cook the rice noodles according to package instructions. Drain well.

3 Preheat a wok or heavy skillet and add oil. Sauté garlic on high heat until it is just beginning to create an aroma. Add rice noodles and stir well, leaving the pan on the heat for less than a minute - just until the noodles are coated with the garlic and oil. Remove noodles from heat and serve with the pepper medley. (See sidebar.)

Yield: approximately 8 servings

CHICKPEA AND COUSCOUS SALAD

The great thing about this recipe is that it takes almost no time to prepare and can be treated as a whole meal. These light Mediterranean flavors are a wonderful meal option, especially during the hot summer months. I love to pack up this salad for picnics or to take to work.

1 pkg (5.6 oz) dry couscous

1 Tbsp olive oil

1 tsp kosher salt

1 can chickpeas (19 oz)

Kosher salt

Freshly ground pepper

1 Tbsp olive oil

2 cloves garlic, minced (see Note)

Zest of 1 lemon

Juice of half a lemon

Less than 1 cup thinly sliced cucumbers

¼ cup chopped fresh parsley or cilantro

1   Cook couscous according to package directions, adding olive oil and kosher salt.

2   Meanwhile, drain chickpeas. Spread them out on a towel. Rub the chickpeas with the palm of your hand to remove the skins. Sprinkle liberally with kosher salt and freshly ground black pepper.

3   Fluff cooked couscous with a fork, then pour into a large bowl and let cool. Add oil, garlic, lemon zest, juice, parsley and chickpeas. Toss to combine.

VARIATION   Add ½ cup feta cheese and toss.

NOTE   If you use the frozen garlic cubes, use at least three. However, try to use fresh garlic when you can.

Yield: approximately 6 servings

SWEET CARROT SALAD

This is such a great salad for Shabbos because you can make it in advance, and it even improves when it sits in the refrigerator. We usually serve it on Shabbos day along with cold cuts and schnitzel. Some people like to add canned pineapple chunks to the salad as well.

8 medium carrots, peeled and trimmed

2 cups orange juice

1 can (11 oz) mandarin oranges plus half the liquid

½ cup golden raisins

½ cup toasted walnuts, as a garnish

1. Shred the carrots finely and add remaining ingredients except nuts. Mix well.

2. Garnish with nuts immediately before serving.

Yield: 4 to 5 servings

CALIFORNIA SALAD

Imitation crab, or surimi, is a product popularly used in sushi, especially California rolls. It can be found in the freezer section of most kosher supermarkets and fish stores. It is sold both as small pieces or longer sticks. For this salad, I prefer the sticks.

Salad:

4 large bell peppers in 4 different colors

10 sticks surimi seafood sticks (approximately)

2 whole scallions, chopped

Kosher salt

Spicy Mayo Dressing:

⅓ cup low-fat mayonnaise

1 Tbsp lemon juice

2 tsp hot sauce (adjust to taste)

½ tsp sugar

1 Tbsp water

1. Dice the peppers and the imitation crab into small, equally sized cubes. (The actual size does not matter, as long as you remain consistent. I prefer the size to be very small because I think it looks nice.)

2. Place all salad ingredients into a bowl and sprinkle very lightly with kosher salt.

3. Mix the dressing ingredients in a bowl, pour over the salad, and mix until evenly coated.

Yield: 8 servings

COUSCOUS SALAD

WITH GRILLED VEGETABLES

This salad is a refreshing combination of many distinct tastes and colors. It is best served at room temperature. If you don't have a grill, the vegetables can easily be roasted in an oven preheated to 450°F.

4 Asian eggplants, cut lengthwise into strips

1 large red bell pepper, cut into wedges

Olive oil

Kosher salt

1 package whole wheat couscous (approx 10 oz)

4 Tbsp chopped fresh parsley

2 Tbsp chopped chives or scallions

4 Tbsp pine nuts, toasted

3 Tbsp fresh lemon juice

4 Tbsp extra-virgin olive oil

2 cloves garlic, crushed

Kosher salt and freshly ground pepper

1   Preheat grill to medium-high heat. (See sidebar.)

2   Coat eggplant and red pepper with olive oil and sprinkle with kosher salt. Spray grill grates generously and grill eggplant and pepper for about 5 minutes on each side. Remove and let cool slightly, then cut into cubes.

3   Cook couscous according to package instructions. Add a bit of olive oil to the water when cooking so the grains don't stick together.

4   Place remaining ingredients along with couscous in a large bowl and toss to combine. Add grilled eggplant and peppers and toss to combine.

NOTE   This salad lasts up to 3 days in the refigerator, making it my number one choice for a do-ahead recipe.

Yield: 8 servings

ORIENTAL SLAW

The eye-catching colors and excellent combination of flavors make this salad a real treat. I got the idea for this salad from Jacob's Catering in Toronto, and I present it here with a few modifications. You can use a julienne cutter or food processor with a large grating attachment to do all the cutting, except for the scallions, which must be done manually.

1 cup edamame (soybeans)

2 mangoes

3 large carrots

3 scallions

3 cups shredded white cabbage (you can use Bodek)

Dressing:

4 Tbsp extra-virgin olive oil

1 tsp low-sodium soy sauce

1 Tbsp freshly ground ginger

6 Tbsp rice vinegar

3 Tbsp light brown sugar

1 tsp salt

½ tsp garlic powder

1   Blanch edamame beans according to package instructions. Place immediately into cold water to stop the cooking after about 4 minutes.

2   Meanwhile, peel and cut mangoes and carrots into julienne shape.

3   Cut the scallions into 2-inch pieces and then cut those pieces into very thin strips. Shred cabbage.

4   Mix together ingredienrs for dressing in a small bowl (you can do this ahead of time.)

5   Combine all salad ingredients just before serving. Toss with dressing.

NOTE   If setting out as appetizer, you can mix the salad with just a few teaspoons of the dressing, and then pour the dressing right before your meal begins.

Garnish with pickled ginger if desired.

Yield: 8 servings

GRILLED EGGPLANT

WITH TOMATOES AND FETA CHEESE

Fresh flavors, salty cheese, and bold balsamic blend together to create a real treat. For a pareve option, omit the feta cheese.

2 small eggplants, sliced crosswise (do not peel)

Extra-virgin olive oil for brushing

Salt and freshly ground black pepper

2 vine-ripened tomatoes, cut into thin wedges

2 tsp capers (optional)

¼ cup crumbled feta cheese

Fresh Italian parsley, for garnishing

Dressing:

2 cloves garlic, minced

1½ Tbsp red wine vinegar

1½ Tbsp balsamic vinegar

½ tsp dried oregano

2 tsp extra-virgin olive oil

¼ tsp freshly ground black pepper

⅛ tsp salt

1 Preheat oven to 450°F.

2 Brush eggplant with olive oil, sprinkle with salt and pepper, and place slices directly onto the rack in your oven using 2 racks. Cover the bottom rack with foil and place eggplant on top one. Otherwise, place an oven liner on the lower rack to catch drips. Let eggplant grill for about 10 minutes, turning slices over halfway through cooking.

3 Meanwhile, combine all the ingredients for the dressing in a bowl.

4 When eggplant is done, cool to room temperature and mix with tomatoes and capers. Toss with dressing, sprinkle with feta cheese on top, and garnish with Italian parsley.

NOTE If you prefer, broil eggplant slices on a broiling pan.

Yield: 5 servings

QUINOA SALAD

My friend Dina made up the recipe for this salad while I was watching her - hence the squirt of honey and squirt of lime. Quinoa is known as the "super grain" and when it is mixed with the right ingredients it really can taste "super."

2 cups water or vegetable broth

1 cup quinoa

1 cup fresh green peas

1 cup mixed colored peppers (yellow, red and/or orange), diced

2 Tbsp chopped scallions

Dressing:

1 tsp toasted sesame oil

1 tsp olive oil

2 tsp soy sauce

½ tsp black pepper

½ tsp salt

Squirt of honey (1 to 2 Tbsp)

Squirt of lime (1 to 2 Tbsp)

1 Bring water or broth to a boil. Place quinoa in a fine-meshed strainer and rinse under cold running water. Rinse until water runs clear; drain well. Add quinoa to boiling liquid, reduce heat and simmer, covered, for 15 minutes.

2 Remove quinoa from heat and let stand covered for 5 minutes. Fluff with a fork. Let cool to room temperature.

3 Dressing: Combine ingredients for dressing in a small bowl and mix well. Stir into quinoa.

4 Add peas, peppers and scallions to quinoa within 2 hours of serving and mix gently to combine.

Yield: 4 servings

QUICK CAPRESE

This is my favorite way to serve tomatoes. I prefer using heirloom tomatoes, because they add beautiful colors and flavor. Vine-ripened tomatoes also work well.

3 heirloom tomatoes, quartered

5 oz fresh mozzarella cheese, sliced (approximately)

¼ cup fresh basil leaves (approximately)

Kosher salt and fresh ground black pepper, for sprinkling

Dressing:

¼ cup good quality olive oil

½ cup basil leaves (approximately)

1   Toss all the salad ingredients together in a bowl or arrange attractively on a large serving platter.

2   Place ingredients for dressing in a blender or food processor and pulse until leaves become small pieces.

3   Pour dressing over salad and serve.

NOTE   If you don't want to use a food processor or blender for the dressing, simply chop the basil leaves very finely and mix into olive oil.

Yield: 4 servings

CELERY ROOT SALAD

This salad is especially great for times when you want to be organized as you can prepare it in advance. It tastes better after being refrigerated for 24 hours! Its crunchy, refreshing taste goes especially well with cold cuts or grilled chicken – hot or cold.

1 small head celery root, peeled

2 Granny Smith apples, unpeeled

1 Tbsp apple juice

2 medium carrots, peeled

¼ cup mayonnaise (regular or light)

2 Tbsp white vinegar (see Note)

2 Tbsp sugar

1 tsp salt dissolved in 1 Tbsp hot water

½ tsp ground black pepper

½ cup salted and toasted sunflower seeds

2 green onions (scallions), green parts only, thinly sliced

1 In a food processor fitted with the grater attachment, grate celery root and transfer it into a large bowl. Then grate apples and add them to the bowl. Add apple juice and mix to combine. Grate carrots and add to mixture.

2 In another bowl, combine mayonnaise, vinegar, sugar, salted water and black pepper and whisk vigorously until smooth.

3 Pour over vegetables, mix and refrigerate overnight. Add sunflower seeds and scallions just before serving and toss to combine.

NOTE For a more intense flavor, use white wine vinegar instead of white vinegar.

Yield: 4 to 6 servings

GREEK PASTA SALAD

This salad takes only moments to make and is full of delicious flavor and bold colors. If you prefer smaller chunks of feta, you can crumble the cheese to a finer consistency.

1 package (10 oz) fusilli or rotini

3 Tbsp extra-virgin olive oil, divided use

8 oz feta cheese (light or regular)

Juice of half a lemon

1 Tbsp dried oregano

½ purple onion, finely shredded

1 cup black olive rings

8 cherry tomatoes, quartered

Salt and freshly ground black pepper

1 Cook pasta according to package directions, and drain well. Place in a large bowl. Add 1 tablespoon extra-virgin olive oil and toss to coat.

2 In a separate bowl, place feta cheese and cut it into small chunks. Add lemon juice, 2 tablespoons olive oil, and oregano. Mix until combined.

3 Add shredded onions, olives and tomatoes to the pasta. Add cheese mixture as well and toss gently to combine. Season with salt and pepper to taste.

Yield: 4 servings

YELLOW BEET SALAD

The recipe can also be used with red beets, but I like using yellow beets because they make less of a mess and don't stain clothing, hands, and tablecloths the way red beets do. This salad should last for a week in the refrigerator, (if it lasts that long)!

6 to 8 yellow beets (approximately)

2 Tbsp vinegar

2 tsp sugar

1 tsp salt

Dressing:

2 Tbsp extra-virgin olive oil

3 Tbsp vinegar

1 ½ Tbsp sugar

2 tsp kosher salt (adjust to taste)

⅛ tsp black pepper

¼ cup finely chopped cilantro leaves, for garnishing

1 Preheat a large pot with enough water to just cover the beets. Add vinegar, sugar, and salt to water (either before or after the water has been heated). Rinse beets well, add to pot, and cook for approximately 30 minutes or until a knife can easily be inserted. Drain water and let beets cool for a few minutes. Peel beets and slice lengthwise. Place in a large bowl.

2 While beets are cooking, mix the ingredients for the dressing in a small bowl. Pour dressing over the sliced beets and let them marinate in the dressing for thirty minutes in the refrigerator before serving. Sprinkle with cilantro leaves when ready to serve.

Yield: 6 servings

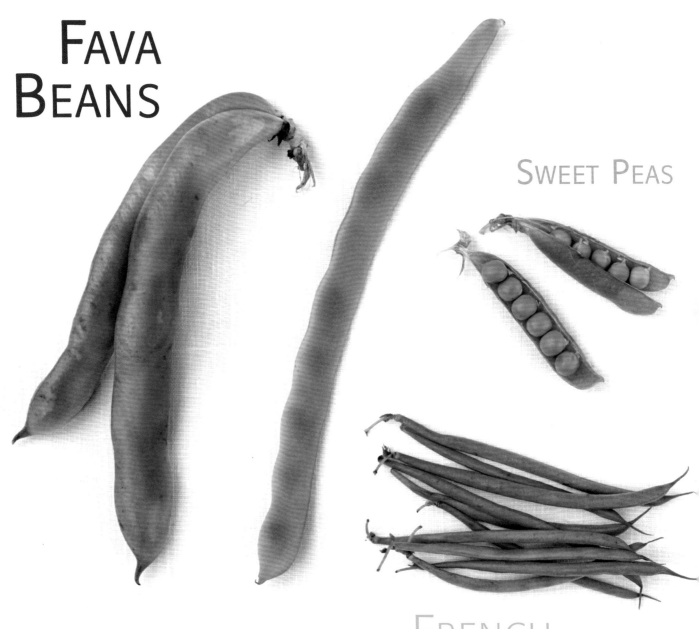

FAVA
BEANS

FLAT BEANS

SWEET PEAS

FRENCH
GREEN
BEANS

breads

soup

salads

meat + poultry

sides

dairy dishes

PAN-SEARED FISH

WITH MANGO SALSA

The bright flavors of these ingredients create a wonderful combination of taste and color that is sure to enhance any meal.

4 fillets of white-fleshed fish such as turbot, sea bass, or tilapia

1 Tbsp light soy sauce

1 tsp fresh ginger juice (see Note)

½ tsp garlic powder

3 Tbsp butter

Kosher salt

Freshly ground black pepper

Salsa:

1 mango, finely diced

1 cup cherry tomatoes, finely diced

1 cup unpeeled English cucumber, diced

1 scallion, finely chopped

Freshly ground black pepper

1 tsp fresh ginger juice

1   Rinse fish and pat dry. Combine soy sauce, ginger juice and garlic powder in a bowl. Marinate fish for approximately 1 hour.

2   Preheat oven to broil.

3   In a heavy-duty frying pan or skillet, melt the butter until clear but not brown. Place fish with flesh facing downward into pan and sear for approximately 2 minutes, until just slightly firm and brown. Sprinkle with salt and pepper.

4   Transfer fish to a 9 x 13-inch baking pan, flesh side up. Broil for about 3 minutes.

5   Combine all the ingredients for the salsa in a bowl and mix. Pour over fish.

NOTE   To make fresh ginger juice: Grate and mince about 3 tablespoons of fresh ginger. Pick up the grated ginger and squeeze it over a bowl until the juice is extracted. (If the ginger is old, it may be dry. You can use the actual minced ginger in this case.)

Yield: 4 servings, based on a 5-ounce portion of fish

FARFALLE

WITH POACHED SALMON AND PEAS

In this light dish, beautiful colors and fresh flavors combine to create a delightful meal.

Boiling salt water

1 tsp olive oil

1 pkg (1 lb) farfalle (bow tie pasta)

2 Tbsp butter, divided use

3 dinner-size skinless salmon fillets

Kosher salt and freshly ground black pepper

¼ cup water

Zest of 1 lemon

1 Tbsp fresh lemon juice

2 Tbsp white wine

10 oz pkg green peas (about 1½ cups, fresh or frozen)

1 tsp cornstarch dissolved in 1 Tbsp cold water

1 Tbsp chopped Italian parsley

1 Heat a large pot of salted boiling water. Add olive oil and cook farfalle until al dente, according to package directions. Drain and mix in 1 tablespoon butter.

2 Meanwhile, rinse salmon and pat dry. Season with salt and pepper. In a saucepan that has a cover, place water, salmon, lemon zest, lemon juice, and white wine. Bring to a simmer over medium heat, cover, and steam for 10 minutes.

3 Add peas and let steam for 3 to 4 minutes. Remove salmon from sauce with a slotted spatula and set aside. Lower the heat slightly.

4 Add dissolved cornstarch to saucepan and stir until sauce begins to thicken. Stir in 1 tablespoon butter. Add to pasta and mix.

5 Gently flake the salmon fillets into small chunks and add to pasta as well. Sprinkle with chopped parsley and serve immediately.

NOTE You can replace the butter with margarine or olive oil to keep this dish pareve.

Yield: 6 servings based on a 3-ounce piece of salmon per person.

FILLET OF SOLE AMANDINE

Here is a classic favorite that is still delicious every time. It takes only minutes to prepare and is a great healthy alternative to breaded fish.

1 cup flour

½ tsp salt

½ tsp black pepper

Juice of 1 lemon

4 fillets of sole

2 to 3 Tbsp butter or margarine

½ cup sliced almonds

1 Combine flour, salt, and pepper on a plate. Place lemon juice in a bowl. Rinse fish and pat dry. Dip each piece into the lemon juice and then into the flour mixture, coating evenly.

2 Melt butter in a heavy skillet over low heat.

3 Spread almonds evenly in the skillet and cook for about 2 minutes. Then place pieces of sole onto the almonds and cook for approximately 3 to 4 minutes over a medium flame (make sure flame is not too high, or almonds will burn). Flip fillets over and cook for another 3 minutes on the second side. Remove from heat. Scrape extra almonds off the bottom of the pan and serve with the fish.

NOTE Margarine can be substituted for the butter to keep this dish pareve.

Yield: 4 servings, based on a 5-ounce portion of fish

TERIYAKI SALMON WRAP

Wraps are another one of those quick and easy meals that have become very popular. Here I have caramelized the onions, but you can also brush them generously with olive oil and grill them in the panini maker.

2 appetizer-size salmon fillets, without skin (6 oz each)

½ cup teriyaki sauce

Caramelized onions (see below)

2 10-inch tortillas (any desired flavor)

3 to 4 pieces romaine lettuce leaves, cut into thin strips

Dressing:

2 Tbsp mayonnaise

2 tsp mustard

1 tsp vinegar

½ tsp chopped basil

Caramelized Onions:

1 large Spanish onion, sliced

3 Tbsp sugar

1 Rinse salmon and pat dry. Marinate in teriyaki sauce in refrigerator for 2 hours or overnight.

2 For the caramelized onions, place onion and sugar in a heavy-bottomed saucepan and let cook over low flame for about 15 minutes, stirring gently every few minutes. Onions are ready when browned.

3 Preheat grill on high and grill marinated salmon for about 3 to 4 minutes on each side.

4 Meanwhile, mix all ingredients for dressing in a small bowl. Spread each tortilla wrap with dressing. Add a handful of shredded lettuce, a salmon fillet, and caramelized onions. Fold in two sides, then roll up to create an envelope effect.

5 Place wrap seam-side down on panini grill and let grill for about 1 minute. Use extra dressing for dipping sauce.

NOTE Use fat-free mayonnaise to make it lower in fat.

Yield: 2 servings

SOLE WITH SPECIAL TOMATO SAUCE

Sole is a fish that is low in fat and high in protein. This recipe has an excellent, if not slightly unusual combination of flavors that you are sure to enjoy.

4 fillets of sole (5 oz each)

½ tsp grilling spice or Montreal steak spice

1 tsp cumin

½ tsp paprika

1 lemon

Sauce:

1 onion, diced

2 plum tomatoes, diced

2 vine-ripened tomatoes, diced

2 Tbsp capers

Juice of half a lemon, freshly squeezed

1 tsp kosher salt

½ tsp freshly ground black pepper

2 Tbsp extra-virgin olive oil (divided use)

1 Rinse sole fillets and pat dry. Mix grilling spices, cumin and paprika together in a small bowl. Cut lemon into wedges.

2 Combine all sauce ingredients in a second bowl. Preheat saucepan with 1 tablespoon oil. Add ingredients for sauce and let cook on medium-low heat, stirring occasionally. Cook until the juices have evaporated and tomatoes are very soft, about 15 to 20 minutes.

3 Meanwhile, preheat a second frying pan with 1 tablespoon extra virgin olive oil (or butter). Once hot, place as many of the sole fillets as will fit in the pan without overlapping, and squeeze a wedge of lemon over them. Cook on one side for about 2 to 3 minutes, then turn them over. Sprinkle both sides of fish with spice mixture while cooking. Cook on the other side until just starting to brown. Remove from heat and pour sauce over fish. Serve warm or at room temperature.

Yield: 4 servings

SESAME SALMON

A gourmet presentation you can easily achieve! The sweet teriyaki sauce and crunchy sesame seeds add a really nice twist to the salmon. The flavored noodles are a tasty and elegant serving idea.

4 appetizer-sized fillets of salmon (skin removed) (6 oz each)

1 cup honey teriyaki sauce

1 cup sesame seeds

3 Tbsp oil

1 pkg (10 oz) cappellini noodles

1 tsp olive oil

1 tsp toasted sesame oil

2 tsp soy sauce

½ tsp black pepper

½ tsp kosher salt

¼ tsp honey

1　Rinse salmon and pat dry. Marinate salmon in honey teriyaki sauce for half an hour in the refrigerator.

2　Roll each piece of marinated salmon in sesame seeds to coat all sides.

3　Preheat oil in a large skillet on medium heat. Place salmon in pan. Let cook for about 4 minutes on one side. Turn salmon over and cook about 3 minutes more. (You can test for readiness by inserting a fork into the center of one piece. If the fish flakes, it is ready.) Place on paper towel to absorb excess oil.

4　Meanwhile, cook capellini according to package directions, adding 1 teaspoon olive oil to the water. Drain and rinse. Add remaining ingredients to pasta and toss.

5　Place a small mound of noodles on the center of each plate and top with a piece of sesame salmon. Serve at room temperature.

NOTE　For a pretty presentation I substiute about 1/3 of the sesame seeds with black sesame seeds.

Yield 4 servings

SALMON QUICHE

What a great way to serve salmon, especially for a lunch meal. A wedge can be placed on each individual plate, with a slice of lemon and a small dollop of mayonnaise or tartar sauce at the side. This is a great way to stretch three servings of salmon into eight pieces servings

1½ lbs salmon fillet (skin on)

1 small lemon

Kosher salt

Freshly ground black pepper

Crust:

1 cup flour

¼ tsp salt

¼ cup oil

¼ cup very cold water

Filling:

½ cup light mayonnaise

2 Tbsp soy milk or milk

3 Tbsp Tofutti Better Than Cream Cheese (or cream cheese)

2 Tbsp flour

3 eggs

3 Tbsp fresh Italian parsley, finely minced

¼ tsp salt

1 Preheat oven to 400°F.

2 Rinse salmon and pat dry. Place salmon in a shallow baking dish and squeeze lemon juice over it. Sprinkle with salt and pepper. Cover tightly and bake for 20 minutes.

3 Meanwhile, make the crust: Mix flour with salt in a bowl, then add oil and mix with a fork. Add water slowly and mix until incorporated. Knead the dough with your hands until very well combined. Roll out the dough and, using your fingers, press into an ungreased 9-inch pie or quiche dish, smoothing and pressing together any holes that may occur.

4 When salmon is done (it may look slightly underbaked) remove the skin and discard. Place salmon in a bowl. Break apart with a fork and let cool.

5 Meanwhile, reset oven temperature to 350°F. Combine all the ingredients for the filling (except the salmon) and mix very well until there are no lumps.

6 Once the salmon has cooled, press on the salmon and drain any juices that may have gathered. (It is important to drain it well so the salmon won't be too watery.) Crumble between your fingers until there are no large chunks left. Add the salmon to the filling and mix until combined.

7 Pour filling mixture into the prepared crust and bake for half an hour. Cut into wedges and serve.

Yield: 8 servings (or wedges)

SPANISH-STYLE FISH

4 whitefish steaks or 4 pieces tilapia

1 Tbsp extra-virgin olive oil (approximately)

2 cloves garlic, crushed

1 (14 oz) can diced tomatoes

1 jalapeno pepper, grated (discard seeds)

3 heaping Tbsp tomato paste

2 tsp sugar

½ orange bell pepper, thinly sliced

½ yellow bell pepper, thinly sliced

½ lb okra, sliced crosswise in 1-inch pieces

1 Preheat oven to 350°F. Rinse fish and pat dry.

2 In a large skillet, sauté the garlic in olive oil until fragrant (not brown). Add the remaining ingredients (except the fish) in the order in which they appear, stirring to combine after each addition. Let cook for about 15 minutes on low heat, or until the peppers and the okra begin to soften slightly. Let sauce cool.

3 Place fish in an oven-safe dish and pour cooled sauce over to cover completely. Cover well and bake for about half an hour.

NOTE I like to add additional peppers to the sauce after it has cooked, right before baking in the oven, to add additional color and texture.

Yield: 4 servings based on a 5 oz portion of fish

THE REBBETZIN'S GEFILTE FISH

This light and fluffy homemade gefilte fish recipe was given to me by Rebbetsin C. Muller. I used to spend many Shabbos afternoons at their home. Years later, searching for that perfect gefilte fish recipe, I knew exactly where to go. This recipe also works for Pesach as well.

2 lbs of ground whitefish

1 medium onion

2 medium carrots

2 eggs

½ cup sugar

White pepper

2 level tsp salt

Add into water:

¼ to ½ cup sugar

3 Tbsp kosher salt

Black pepper

2 onions, sliced

2 large carrots

1 For fish mixture, grate carrots and onions very finely. Place in a large bowl.

2 Add fish, eggs, sugar and white pepper. Mix well, add salt and mix again. The salt pulls together the mixture.

3 Place 2 pieces of parchment paper (about 18 inches long) on a flat surface and make them slightly wet by wiping them with a wet cloth. Place ½ of mixture onto the centre of each piece of paper and roll paper around the mixture forming a log, twisting at the ends to seal.

4 In a large pot, combine about 1½ inches of water, sugar, salt, pepper, sliced onions and whole carrots. Bring to a boil.

5 Place logs into boiling water and cover and simmer for 45 minutes. Remove the paper from around the fish and let simmer for 45 minute more. Serve cold.

TIP Use small fancy cookie cutters to cut out fancy shapes from the cooked carrots. Use as a garnish on the fish slices when serving.

Yield: 2 average size logs (about 16 servings)

BREADED SALMON SKEWERS

WITH GRILLED VEGETABLES

This salmon dish is wildly popular in our family. I have served it on skewers, tossed it into a pasta salad, or served it on a bed of lettuce. Here is my all-time favorite way to serve it as an appetizer. (Please note that the marinade and the sauce are actually the same, so you can use half for the marinade and reserve some for drizzling.)

4 fillets salmon (6 oz each), thinly sliced (no skin)

1 cup seasoned corn flake crumbs

Marinade/Sauce:

4 Tbsp mustard

4 Tbsp honey

½ cup extra-virgin olive oil

2 Tbsp fresh lemon juice

Grilled Vegetables:

2 large red onions

3 medium bell peppers (any preferred colors)

¼ cup olive oil

Kosher salt

Freshly ground black pepper

1 Rinse salmon and pat dry. Cut into approximately 1-inch chunks. Place crumbs in a resealable plastic bag.

2 Combine mustard, honey, olive oil and lemon juice in a bowl and mix. Reserve half to use later as a sauce. Place pieces of salmon into remaining marinade and mix to coat all sides. Cover well. Refrigerate half an hour or overnight.

3 Preheat oven to 375°F.

4 Roll each piece of salmon in corn flake crumbs and place on a baking sheet (or baking dish) lined with parchment paper. Bake for 12 minutes. Allow to cool. Before serving, place 2 to 3 pieces of salmon onto toothpicks or a wooden skewer by piercing each piece in the center.

5 Meanwhile, prepare grilled vegetables. Preheat oven to broil.

6 Thinly slice the red onion into round discs and the peppers into round flower-shaped slices. (To make pepper flowers, cut away the stem from the top of the pepper and then remove seeds from the center. Cut slices of pepper clockwise into rings.)

7 Place onions and pepper rounds on a baking sheet lined with parchment paper and drizzle with olive oil. Sprinkle with kosher salt and pepper. Broil for 12 minutes or until starting to blacken. To serve, pile the onion and peppers into a small mound in the center of the plate and prop a salmon skewer up against it. Drizzle with reserved marinade. Can be served warm or at room temperature.

NOTE You can prepare the marinated salmon pieces ahead of time and freeze them unbaked. Bake the salmon the day you are serving them and serve at room temperature.

Yield: 4 servings as a main dish or 6 to 8 servings as an appetizer

SCALLIONS

GARLIC

SHALLOT

RED
ONION

PEARL
ONION

breads

soup

salads

fish

meat + poultry

sides

dairy dishes

LAST MINUTE MIAMI RIBS

This is one of my favorite last minute, never-fail sauces and tastes terrific on Miami ribs. It couldn't be simpler and the orange juice gives it a nice citrusy twist. You might want to add some sliced onions to the pan under the meat, but if you are in a rush, it tastes great without it.

12 Miami-style ribs (see Note)

Sauce:
¼ cup low-sodium soy sauce

¼ cup orange juice

¼ cup ketchup

¼ cup honey

1 tsp garlic powder

1 Preheat oven to 300°F.

2 Place meat in the bottom of a greased baking dish. Do not pile the ribs more than 2 high.

3 Mix all ingredients for sauce together in a bowl and pour evenly over meat, making sure all the meat is covered with sauce. Cover pan tightly with aluminum foil.

4 Bake for 2 hours.

Note Miami ribs are beef short ribs (flanken) that have been sliced into thin strips across the bone by the butcher. They're about ½-inch thick.

Yield: 4 to 6 servings

PICKLED TONGUE IN TOMATO SAUCE WITH PINEAPPLE

1 pickled tongue (about 4 lbs)

2 Tbsp flour

2 Tbsp oil

2 14-oz cans tomato sauce

2½ Tbsp brown sugar

1 Tbsp lemon juice

Wedge of lemon peel

1 14-oz can pineapple chunks, drained

This sauce works very nicely with any pickled meat. For this recipe, I used pickled tongue because it is extremely soft and very popular with my family.

1 Cook tongue in a large pot full of water for about 2½ to 3 hours. Discard water and peel outer skin of tongue while still quite hot. Let cool completely, and then slice.

2 Mix flour and oil together in a saucepan. Add tomato sauce, brown sugar, lemon juice, and lemon peel. Cook over gentle heat for about 10 minutes, stirring occasionally. Add pineapple and cook for 5 minutes more.

3 Preheat oven to 350°F. Place sliced tongue into a serving dish and pour the sauce over the meat. Warm up together for about 20 to 30 minutes.

Yield: 8 servings

COLORFUL STUFFED VEAL

This is a special dish for a special occasion. It makes a very elegant main dish, and the best thing about this recipe is that it freezes beautifully.

1 veal neck with pocket (5 to 6 lbs)

1 lemon

Spice Rub:

1 tsp black pepper

1 tsp Kosher salt

½ Tbsp oil

1 clove garlic, minced

½ tsp paprika

Stuffing:

1 medium onion, cut in chunks

3 cloves garlic

¼ cup chopped fresh Italian parsley

1 red bell pepper, divided in half

1 lb ground chicken

½ tsp salt

½ tsp freshly ground black pepper

½ tsp sugar

1 extra-large egg

⅔ cup bread crumbs

1 To prepare meat, rub it all over with the juice of the lemon. Rinse with water and pat dry with a paper towel, both inside and out.

2 For the spice rub, mix all ingredients together in a small bowl.

3 To make stuffing, place onion, garlic, parsley, and half a red pepper into a food processor and coarsely chop. Place in a large mixing bowl and add ground chicken, salt, pepper and sugar. Mix well. Add egg and breadcrumbs and mix again.

4 Place meat in a large roasting pan and rub with spice rub, covering all surfaces as evenly as possible.

5 Cut remaining half of bell pepper into long thin strips. Place stuffing into the cavity of the meat, placing a red pepper strip horizontally every few inches. Close ends of meat around stuffing. Cover pan well.

6 Bake at 400°F for the first 30 minutes, then reduce heat to 350° F and bake for 2 hours. Remove and let cool to room temperature before slicing.

Yield: 10 to 12 servings

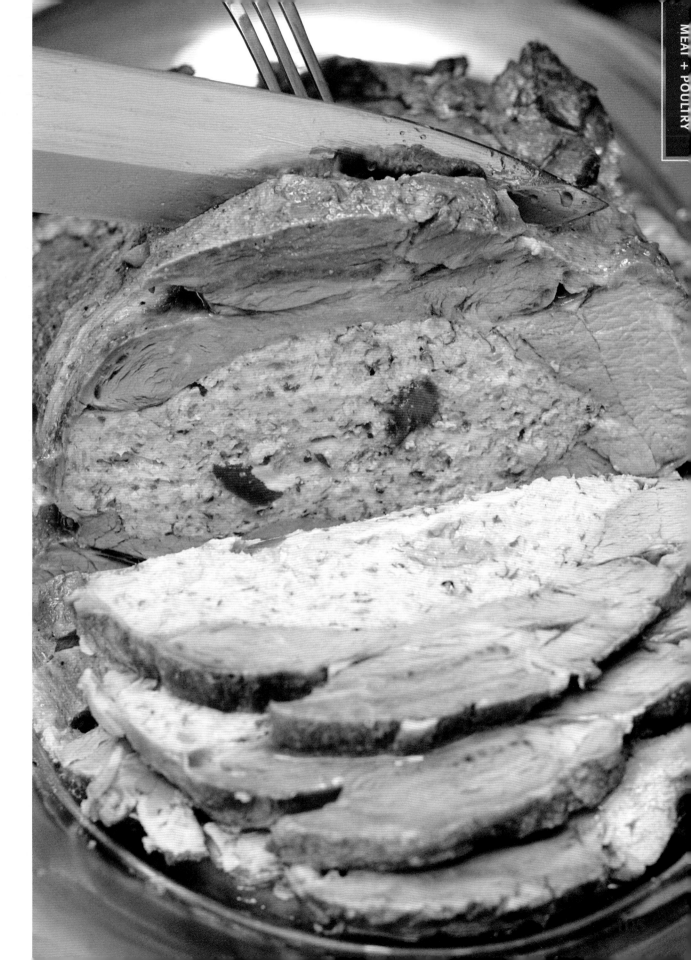

MARINATED SCHNITZEL

WITH PEPPER AND PORTABELLA SAUCE

This recipe works with either chicken breast or chicken thigh meat. (Whenever I make schnitzel, I try to use dark meat (chicken thighs) that have been deboned. The schnitzel comes out more tender, and it's easier for little children to chew. You can freeze the schnitzel once it has been breaded then defrost and cook it. However, the sauce is best when made fresh.

4 chicken cutlets, either breast or thigh (deboned), cut into finger-size pieces

1 cup barbecue sauce

1 cup bread crumbs

Olive oil for frying

Sauce:

1 onion, chopped

4 large portabella mushrooms, cleaned and finely chopped

1 red bell pepper, finely chopped

1 Tbsp kosher salt

Freshly ground black pepper

Chopped fresh parsley or chives for garnish

1 Marinate chicken pieces in barbecue sauce in a large bowl or resealable bag. Refrigerate for half an hour (or overnight).

2 Shake off excess barbecue sauce from chicken and dip all sides into the bread crumbs, coating evenly. (You can freeze the chicken at this point.)

3 When ready to use, preheat a large frying pan with oil and fry chicken on both sides on medium heat until golden brown and cooked through — about 4 minutes on each side. Drain excess oil on paper towels.

4 To make sauce: In a wok or medium saucepan, preheat olive oil on medium heat and add onions. Once onions have become transparent, add peppers and let cook for about 2 minutes. Add mushrooms, then season with salt and pepper. Saute on low heat until vegetables are just turning soft.

5 Top schnitzel with vegetable sauce and garnish with fresh parsley. Serve with cooked brown rice or wild rice pilaf.

TIP For a lower-fat version, bake the chicken cutlets in a pan that has been smeared with oil. Cover breaded chicken cutlets with vegetable sauce and bake covered at 350°F for 30 minutes (longer for larger cutlets).

Yield: 4 to 6 servings

CHUNKY MEAT SAUCE DINNER

WITH SPAGHETTI

Here is an example of a supper you can prepare in about 15 to 20 minutes (plus cooking time), using basic ingredients. I chop the vegetables into very fine pieces so the kids won't notice they are there. And it freezes really well!

1 large onion

3 carrots

2 zucchini

½ red bell pepper

1 Tbsp oil

2 lbs ground meat (extra lean)

1 jar (3 cups) marinara sauce (I use the one with roasted garlic)

1½ Tbsp sugar

1½ tsp salt

Freshly ground black pepper

2 bay leaves

1 pkg (16 oz) spaghetti

1   Cut the onion, carrots, zucchini and bell pepper into chunks. Place in the food processor fitted with the steel blade. (If your family will actually eat vegetables in larger pieces, consider just shredding them.)

2   In a very large saucepan or large shallow pot, heat oil. Pour in all vegetables and sauté for 5 minutes on medium heat, stirring constantly. Add meat (I am usually running late, so I brown the meat in another saucepan and then add it to the vegetables to speed up the cooking time). Sauté until meat is brown, then stir in marinara sauce and seasonings. Cover and simmer about 30 to 45 minutes, stirring occasionally. Remove bay leaves from sauce and discard.

3   While meat sauce is cooking, boil water in a large pasta pot. Add salt to taste and cook spaghetti according to package directions (break in half if you have young customers). Drain well. Serve spaghetti and meat sauce together (wear bibs for this one!).

Yield: 6 servings (very approximate)

ROCK CORNISH HENS

WITH WHITE WINE GLAZE

This dish is especially tasty and can be put out very nicely on a platter when serving guests. Each guest receives one whole bird or half, depending on their size. I developed this recipe especially for the meal eaten on the Holiday of Purim, in keeping with the theme of wine.

4 Cornish hens

2 Tbsp extra-virgin olive oil

Kosher salt and freshly ground black pepper

¾ cup dry white wine

¾ cup homemade chicken soup

1 tsp Dijon mustard

Juice of half a lemon

1 Preheat oven to 400°F.

2 To butterfly the Cornish hens, cut out the backbone completely, using sharp poultry scissors to cut on either side of it (the backbone is attached to the neck). Flatten the Cornish hens by pressing the centers down. Place skin-side up in a greased roasting pan. Rub skin with olive oil and sprinkle with salt and pepper. Bake for 35 minutes, uncovered.

3 Meanwhile, in a heavy saucepan, bring wine and chicken soup to a simmer and let cook down until reduced to half the amount. Add mustard and lemon juice and stir until combined and just beginning to thicken. Remove from heat.

4 When Cornish hens are done, remove from oven and brush with glaze (also reserve some for serving). Return Cornish hens to oven for 5 to 6 minutes before serving. Pour any leftover sauce onto the hens before serving.

NOTE You can make these 3 hours in advance. Just return them to the oven for the last 5 to 6 minutes right before serving.

SERVING SUGGESTION You may want to pile the poultry onto a bed of rice and mix the extra gravy into the rice. Garnish with fresh Italian (flat leaf) parsley.

Yield: 4 to 8 servings, depending on size

SPECIAL OCCASION MEAT

This recipe works well with any good cut of meat, but my personal preferences are standing rib roast, or on a first or second fillet.

3 large onions, sliced

6 cloves garlic, peeled

2 stalks celery, chopped

Standing rib roast (with or without the bone), 5 to 7 lbs

2 tsp freshly ground black pepper

3 Tbsp vinegar

2 Tbsp extra-virgin olive oil

¼ cup honey

8 to 10 cloves (approximately)

6 bay leaves (approximately)

1 bottle dry red wine (750 ml, about 3 cups)

1 Place onions, garlic, and celery on the bottom of a large greased Pyrex baking dish or Dutch oven. Place meat on top. Sprinkle meat with black pepper; then pour vinegar, olive oil, honey, and cloves onto the meat. With gloved hands, smear the vinegar, olive oil, honey, and cloves evenly all over the meat. Add bay leaves and red wine to the dish. Cover and marinate for 2 hours or overnight in the refrigerator.

2 Preheat oven to 300°F. Make sure the meat is very well covered and bake for 4 to 6 hours, depending on the size of the meat. (If the meat has a bone, you can increase cooking time to 6 hours.) Calculate 45 minutes per lb as your cooking time. Let cool completely before slicing.

3 To finish the gravy, remove the bay leaves and any cloves you can easily find, and puree the vegetables with an immersion blender. You can choose to reheat the gravy separately or in the same pan with the meat.

NOTE To keep the cooked roast warm, wrap the pot in a large towel to insulate it and leave it on the countertop until serving time.

Yield: calculate ½ lb meat per person without the bone or ¾ lb per person with the bone

PEPPER STEAK STIR-FRY

WITH MUSHROOMS AND BOK CHOY

This wonderful combination of vegetables and meat creates a dish with terrific presentation and taste. The bok choy adds both flavor and color. I like to serve this over a bed of rice for a main dish, or with a scoop of rice for an appetizer.

1 lb pepper steak, cut in strips

Extra-virgin olive oil for sauteing

1 large onion, diced
½ red bell pepper, thinly sliced
3 portabella mushrooms, sliced
6 to 7 shiitake mushrooms, sliced
10 button mushrooms, sliced
1 head baby bok choy, leaves shredded

Marinade:

1 Tbsp extra-virgin olive oil
1 Tbsp low-sodium soy sauce
2½ tsp brown sugar
2 cloves garlic, minced

1   Combine the ingredients for the marinade in a bowl. Add pepper steak and mix thoroughly. Let marinate for 20 minutes.

2   Heat a wok and 2 tablespoons olive oil. Sauté onions on medium heat until transparent; then add peppers and saute over high heat for 2 to 3 minutes. Pour onions and peppers into a large bowl.

3   Stir-fry all the mushrooms for approximately 3 minutes, until soft and fragrant. (Add more oil as needed.) Add shredded bok choy, and cook 30 seconds longer. Pour mushrooms and bok choy into the bowl with the sauteéd peppers.

4   Place meat and marinade in the wok and stir-fry meat until cooked through, about 4 to 5 minutes.

5   Add cooked vegetables back into wok and toss thoroughly. Serve warm on a bed of rice, sprinkled with kosher salt and freshly ground black pepper.

Yield: 4 servings

CHICKEN AND MUSHROOM APPETIZER

This dish can be served either warm or cold. I like to serve it with plum sauce alongside or as a great addition to a coldcut platter.

2 lbs boneless chicken thighs (approximately)

1/3 lb brown or baby portabella mushrooms

2 Tbsp extra-virgin olive oil, divided use

2 cloves minced garlic

1/4 cup seasoned bread crumbs

2 Tbsp freshly chopped parsley

Duck sauce for brushing

1 Preheat oven to 350°F. Rinse chicken and pat dry. Trim any excess fat from chicken pieces and discard.

2 Pulse mushrooms in a food processor until finely chopped.

3 Heat 1 Tbsp olive oil in a skillet. Add garlic and sauté until fragrant but not brown. Add mushrooms and saute gently until tender. Remove skillet from heat and stir in bread crumbs and parsley. Let cool.

4 Spray a small loaf pan (8 x 4-inches) with non-stick spray. Place a layer of chicken on the bottom of the pan, using about half the chicken. (Pack it tightly because the chicken will shrink as it cooks.) Spoon mushroom filling on top of the chicken and spread it evenly. Place remaining chicken pieces on top of filling, making the top layer as level as possible. (You can overlap chicken pieces slightly.)

5 Cover well and bake for 1 hour.

6 Remove pan from oven. Pour off all the fat and juices and discard them. Brush the top layer of chicken with duck sauce and cook uncovered about 5 minutes more.

7 Remove pan from oven and let cool for about 20 minutes. Cover again and refrigerate about 3 to 4 hours. It should be completely cold before you slice it. Slice and serve cold or reheat it gently if you prefer.

Yield: 8 servings

HONEY GARLIC ROASTED CHICKEN

WITH VEGETABLES

The most cost-effective way to purchase chicken in its whole form. Roasting the chicken with a few added vegetables makes a healthy, tasty, all-in-one dinner that you never get tired of.

1 3 lb chicken, rinsed and patted dry

3 Tbsp extra-virgin olive oil, divided use

Kosher salt and freshly ground black pepper

2 fennel bulbs, cored, stalks discarded, cut into wedges

2 carrots, peeled and cut into sticks

1½ to 2 lbs baby red potatoes, cut in half

2 cloves garlic, minced

2 Tbsp honey

1 Preheat oven to 450°F.

2 To butterfly the chicken, cut out the backbone completely using sharp poultry scissors on either side of it (the backbone is attached to the neck).

3 Place the chicken on a rack positioned above a foil-lined roasting pan. Rub skin with olive oil and sprinkle with 1 tablespoon salt and pepper. Place fennel, carrots, and potatoes on the lined bottom of the roasting pan.

4 In a small bowl, combine garlic, honey, and 1 tablespoon olive oil. Smear over chicken and toss with vegetables. Add an additional tablespoon of olive oil to vegetables and toss again to combine. Roast uncovered for 50 to 55 minutes.

5 Baste chicken with pan juices and stir the vegetables halfway through. When done, cover loosely with foil and let rest for 10 minutes.

NOTE To check chicken for doneness, try piercing chicken between the breast and leg. When juices run clear, the chicken is done.

Yield: 4 servings

APRICOT CHICKEN SKEWERS

Grilled apricots are somehow tart and sweet at the same time, making them a perfect accompaniment to grilled chicken. Soak your skewers in water before using to avoid burning, or, alternatively, use metal skewers.

1 lb fresh apricots, halved and pitted

1 purple onion, cut into small wedges

1 to 2 lbs skinless, boneless chicken breast or thighs

Marinade:

Juice of half a lemon

1 tsp low-sodium soy sauce

½ tsp black pepper

½ tsp garlic powder

½ tsp ground ginger

1 Rinse chicken and pat dry. Cut chicken into 1-inch squares. Mix all ingredients for marinade in a bowl. Add chicken and toss to coat. Let marinate for a half hour.

2 Place chicken, apricots and onion wedges onto skewers, alternating as you go. Fill skewers a bit more than halfway.

3 Preheat BBQ to medium heat or about 350°F and coat grill generously with non-stick spray or oil. Cook kebobs on each side for about 4 minutes or until chicken is cooked through.

NOTE Try to make sure the pieces of the chicken are not too big; if they are, it will take too long for them to cook and the apricots may fall apart.

Yield: 4 servings

SAVORY GRILLED CHICKEN

The sauce is a nice change from standard barbeque sauces and marinades. It is low in fat and high in taste.

1 medium onion, finely chopped or grated

2 cloves garlic, minced

2 Tbsp olive oil

¼ tsp chili powder or crushed red pepper flakes

¼ tsp ground cumin

¼ tsp paprika

6 medium skinless, boneless chicken breast halves

Shredded lettuce (optional)

Chopped tomato (optional)

Avocado slices (optional)

1 In a small saucepan, cook onion and garlic in olive oil over medium heat until tender. Stir in the chili powder, cumin, and paprika. Cook for 1 minute.

2 Rinse chicken; pat dry with paper towels. Brush half the onion mixture over chicken.

3 Preheat BBQ to medium heat. Grill chicken, uncovered, directly over medium heat, for 6 minutes. Turn chicken over and brush with remaining onion mixture. Grill for 6 to 8 minutes more or until chicken is tender and no longer pink. (If you prefer to broil the chicken, place chicken on the rack of a broiler pan. Broil chicken 5 to 6 inches from the heat for 10 to 12 minutes, turning once and brushing with remaining onion mixture.)

4 Serve with shredded lettuce, chopped tomato, and avocado slices, if desired.

Yield: 6 servings

STEAK SANDWICH

WITH CARAMELIZED ONIONS AND PEPPERS

A skirt steak is a long, thin cut of meat that is a great size for sandwiches. It tends to be a bit tougher than other steak cuts, but it is very flavorful and relatively inexpensive. Slice it against the grain for the best results. The marinade doubles as a sauce for the onions and peppers as well.

1 to 1 ½ lbs skirt steak, rinsed and patted dry

1 tsp black pepper

½ tsp Kosher salt

1 red bell pepper, sliced

1 Vidalia onion, sliced

Marinade:

⅓ cup brown sugar, lightly packed

¼ cup teriyaki sauce

1 Tbsp ketchup

1 Tbsp vinegar

1 Tbsp olive oil

Fresh baguette slices or rolls of your choice

1 Combine all ingredients for the marinade in a small bowl. Season skirt steak with black pepper and salt. Place skirt steak into a resealable bag and pour in half the marinade. Let marinate half an hour or overnight, in the refrigerator.

2 Meanwhile, put other half of the marinade into a saucepan, add peppers and onions, and mix. Cook over low heat, stirring occasionally, for about half hour or until onions are soft and caramelized. (Do not turn heat too high or sugar will begin to burn.)

3 Preheat grill to high. Grill skirt steak on both sides for approximately 3 to 5 minutes per side for medium rare. Brush steak with additional marinade while it is on the grill.

4 Remove steak from the grill and let rest for 5 minutes before cutting. Thinly slice steak at an angle, against the grain, or cut into large pieces and place between bread slices. Add caramelized onions and peppers, and enjoy.

Yield: 4 servings

PICKLED MEAT

WITH MANGO SAUCE

This is my mother-in-law's famous yom tov dish that has become a popular family favorite over the years. She always makes it with a pickled kolachel, but you can try it with other pickled meats as well.

Pickled kolachel, brisket or other boneless roast (about 4 lbs)

2 Tbsp oil

2 Tbsp flour

3 cups mango juice (I like the Ceres brand)

1 can apricot halves, drained (15.25 oz)

¼ cup sugar

1 Tbsp lemon juice

Peel of lemon wedge

1   Fill a large pot with water and bring to a boil.

2   Gently rinse the pickled kolachel roast under running water and place into the boiling water. Let cook about 2 hours or until the meat is tender and cooked through. Remove from the pot and cool. Slice thinly with a sharp knife.

3   In a saucepan, mix the oil and flour until combined. Add the remaining ingredients except meat and cook on very low heat until the sauce is the consistency of a thicker syrup. Cool sauce and remove lemon peel. Add the meat to the pot and warm gently, stirring occasionally.

4   If making in advance, store the meat and sauce separately. When ready to serve, pour the mango sauce into a saucepan and gently heat. Place the meat in the saucepan and cook together until ready to serve.

NOTE   If you can't find mango juice, orange-mango juice can be substituted.

Yield: 8 servings

OUT-STANDING RIB ROAST

This recipe is truly outstanding! I had guests over the first time I tried it and they told me that the aroma alone was worth coming for. (And I thought people came for the company!) Try timing this recipe according to when the meal is scheduled to be served. It is best to start about 4 hours before you are ready to serve.

Rub:

½ cup flour

3 Tbsp chicken soup mix (choose a brand that doesn't contain MSG)

1 Tbsp garlic powder

2 Tbsp dry mustard powder

1 tsp salt

2 tsp freshly ground black pepper

Standing rib roast (any size)

2 Tbsp extra-virgin olive oil

10 onions, sliced

6 cloves garlic, peeled

¾ cup red wine

1   Preheat oven to 350°F.

2   Combine all ingredients for the rub in a bowl and mix well. Smear meat all over with the rub, making sure to cover it completely.

3   Pour olive oil into the bottom of a large Dutch oven and add sliced onions and garlic. Pour red wine over them.

4   Place seasoned roast, bone-side up, on top of the onions.

5   Place in the oven uncovered for about 2 to 2½ hours, depending on how big the roast is (2 to 3 bones should take about 2 hours).

6   Cover the pot once the roast is done and turn off the oven. Let the roast sit for about half hour before serving. If you want to use your oven for other things, wrap the pot in a large towel to insulate it and keep warm on your countertop.

7   When ready to serve, remove bone(s) and cut slices across the grain. Serve with the onion gravy.

Yield: allow ½ to ¾ lb meat per person

ORANGE GLAZED CHICKEN

The orange flavor dresses up your everyday chicken, making it a wonderful choice for a special meal. The glazed orange slices are a lovely garnishing idea. Why not add them to a rice side dish as well!

1 whole chicken (3½ to 4 lbs) (or 1 chicken, cut in 6 pieces)

1 navel orange, sliced crosswise into rounds

1 Tbsp extra-virgin olive oil

Kosher salt

Freshly ground black pepper

Glaze:

¼ cup orange jam or apricot jam

1 tsp ground fresh ginger (or ½ tsp dried ginger)

2 tsp soy sauce

2 tsp fresh lemon juice

Glazed Oranges (optional):

2 Tbsp oil

¼ cup corn syrup

1 Tbsp honey

2 to 3 seedless oranges (or Clementine oranges), thinly sliced

Preheat oven to 375°F. If using a whole chicken, butterfly it as directed below.

Grease a baking dish large enough to fit the flattened chicken (about 10 inches round). Place a layer of orange slices in the bottom of the dish. Place chicken on top, skin side up. Rub chicken skin with olive oil and sprinkle with salt and pepper. Cover well and bake for one hour.

Meanwhile, combine all ingredients for glaze in a small bowl.

After chicken has cooked for an hour, remove from oven and spread glaze evenly all over skin. You can add glazed oranges randomly on top of the skin (optional). Cover again and bake 35 to 40 minutes longer.

Preheat oven to 450°F and roast chicken uncovered 3 or 4 minutes.

For Glazed Oranges, place oil, corn syrup and honey into a saucepan and mix well. Add orange slices and bring to a simmer. Make sure oranges are coated on all sides (you may have to flip them over) and let simmer gently about 20 minutes.

Remove oranges from pan with a fork and place on parchment paper until ready to use.

HOW TO BUTTERFLY A CHICKEN Place chicken, breast side-down and with the tail towards you, on a flat surface. Beginning at one side of the tail, cut through skin, meat and bones to the neck end with poultry scissors. Repeat on the other side of the tail. Lift out backbone (add it when you make your chicken soup). Turn chicken over, laid out flat. Press down on the chicken breast to flatten it.

Yield: 5 servings

NOKEDLI CHICKEN

WITH VEGETABLES

Mrs. Chavi Neumann, a native of Hungary, was gracious enough to share her expertise on making this well-loved, old-time favorite. (You might know this dish as a family tradition called "knokerlach" or "nockerly.") She transmitted the recipe with instructions like, "for every egg you use, add half an eggshell full of seltzer," and "add enough flour to make the batter thick enough to pour." While all of this made perfect sense, I thought that readers might want more specific measurements than that, so while Mrs. Neumann poured, I stood by with a measuring spoon and recorded the "handfuls" as accurately as possible. A special thank you to Aviva for hosting the demo!

2 Tbsp oil
2 large onions, chopped
1 clove garlic, minced
2 sticks celery, minced
2 carrots, finely sliced
1 tsp + ½ Tbsp sweet paprika
1½ tsp kosher salt
1 tsp freshly ground black pepper
6 chicken-leg quarters

Nokedli batter:
4 eggs
8 Tbsp seltzer
¼ tsp ground black pepper
¼ tsp salt
1¾ cups flour

1 Preheat oil in a large, wide pot that has a lid. Sauté the onions, garlic, celery, carrots, 1 teaspoon paprika, salt, and pepper, until beginning to soften. Add chicken (skin side down) and let cook for about 2 to 3 minutes. Turn chicken over and add enough water to partially cover the chicken.

2 Cover and let cook over medium heat for about 1 hour. Add additional half-tablespoon of paprika and cook for 30 to 45 minutes more, until tender.

3 Meanwhile, make Nokedli batter by combining the eggs, seltzer, and spices in a bowl. Beat with a whisk and slowly add flour, constantly beating the mixture to dissolve any lumps. Refrigerate batter for 15 minutes.

4 When the chicken is cooked, uncover and increase heat to high, so that the liquid is brought to a gentle boil. Drop batter into the water, a teaspoonful (or less) at a time, and let cook for 3 minutes.

TIP For a low-fat version, remove skin and fat from chicken before cooking.

Mrs. Neumann showed us how to make this dish in a pressure cooker, too. Add a little less water to the pot in Step 1 and remaining paprika. Reduce the total cooking time for the chicken in Step 2 to 15 minutes. Let the closed pot rest for 5 minutes, and submerge the whole pot in cold water before opening. Then bring cooking liquid to a boil again and add Nokedli batter.

Yield: 6 servings

ASIAN
EGGPLANT

BABY
ENGLISH
CUCUMBER

PLUM
TOMATO

EGGPLANT

EGGPLANT

CHERRY
TOMATO

CHILI
PEPPE

JALAPENO
PEPPER

BELL
PEPPER

ZUCCHINI

PATTYPAN

HEIRLOOM
TOMATO

breads

soup

salads

fish

meat + poultry

sides

dairy dishes

SPICED BUTTERNUT SQUASH CUBES

This side dish takes approximately 15 minutes to prepare, yet looks pretty and is quite filling. A great idea for low-carb dieters.

1 large butternut squash

3 Tbsp extra-virgin olive oil

Kosher salt

Freshly ground black pepper

½ cup chopped walnuts, toasted

¼ cup Italian parsley leaves, chopped

Zest of half an orange

Dash of freshly ground nutmeg

1 Peel butternut squash and remove seeds. Cut into 1-inch cubes.

2 Heat a large pan or heavy skillet and add olive oil. Place butternut squash cubes into pan, sprinkle with kosher salt and freshly ground black pepper, and sauté, tossing every few minutes to ensure that all sides get cooked. Let cook until soft, but not falling apart — about 15 to 20 minutes on medium heat.

3 Remove from heat and add walnuts, chopped parsley, orange zest, and dash of nutmeg. Mix to coat and serve immediately.

Yield: 6 servings

BUTTERNUT SQUASH KUGEL

This recipe is so versatile that if you are pressed for time, it can be made with frozen sweet potatoes and butternut squash and tastes equally delicious.

Filling:

1 large butternut squash (See Note)

7 large sweet potatoes (See Note)

½ cup soy milk

2 Tbsp oil

2 eggs

6 Tbsp sugar

Pinch of salt

1 tsp pumpkin pie spice

Topping:

¼ cup white sugar

⅓ cup brown sugar, lightly packed

½ cup flour

¼ cup margarine (½ stick)

¼ cup ground filberts or walnuts

½ cup chopped toasted pecans

1 Preheat oven to 350°F. Spray a 10-inch round oven-to-table baking dish with nonstick spray.

2 Peel squash and cut in cubes, discarding seeds. Peel sweet potatoes and cut in cubes. Cook in boiling salted water until soft, about 15 to 20 minutes. Drain thoroughly.

3 Place all ingredients for filling of kugel into a large bowl and mix vigorously until completely smooth, or use an immersion blender. Pour filling into baking dish.

4 Place all topping ingredients except toasted pecans in a large bowl and crumble with the tips of your fingers until fine crumbs form. Spread crumbs out on a baking sheet lined with parchment paper and bake for 10 minutes.

5 Remove toasted crumbs from oven, let cool for a few minutes, then sprinkle on top of prepared kugel filling.

6 Sprinkle toasted pecans evenly over the top of the kugel and bake for 35 minutes, on a lower rack in the oven (so the top doesn't burn). Serve warm.

NOTE Substitute 2 (14 oz each) bags frozen butternut squash cubes and 1 (14 oz) bag frozen sweet potato cubes. Defrost and pat dry with paper towels. Continue as directed in Step 3.

Yield: 8 servings

PESTO
STIR-FRY

This is a great side dish which uses my favorite herb to create a delicious stir-fry pesto combination. Try to make this dish as close to serving time as possible, though the pesto can be made up to 2 days in advance and kept refrigerated. Note that the ingredients are all vegetables that don't have to be peeled, so they are easy to prep in advance. Serve hot or at room temperature.

3 Tbsp extra-virgin olive oil

2 cloves garlic, crushed

¾ lb button or brown mushrooms, sliced

1 pint grape tomatoes

1 lb sugar snap peas

1½ tsp kosher salt

¾ tsp freshly ground black pepper

Pesto:

½ cup fresh basil leaves (approximately)

½ cup pine nuts

½ cup extra-virgin olive oil

1   In the bottom of a wok or deep frying pan, heat olive oil at medium-high heat. Add crushed garlic and sauté for about 1 minute, until garlic becomes fragrant. Add mushrooms and sauté until they are beginning to soften, about 2 minutes.

2   Add tomatoes and sugar snap peas and mix constantly. Sprinkle with salt and pepper. Cook snow peas for only about 2 to 3 minutes. They should turn a bright shade of green and retain their crispiness.

3   For the pesto, combine all ingredients in a food processor fitted with a steel blade attachment. Pulse until very fine.

4   Remove stir fry from heat and toss with pesto dressing to coat.

Yield: 12 servings

YUCCA FRIES

If you have never heard of a yucca root you are probably not alone. I once ate these in a restaurant in Manhattan and I had to know what they were, I did my research so I can now share them with you! Also known as cassava, yucca has a white starchy flesh which in my opinion tastes a lot like a potato with a bit of a chestnut flavor. Yucca or cassava is often used in African and Asian countries, and is therefore usually readily available in Chinese fruit stores, but is often stocked in major supermarkets as well.

3 to 4 yucca
Oil for frying
Kosher salt for sprinkling

1 Bring to a boil a large pot of salted water. Peel and cut yucca into generous wedges. Cook for 8 to 10 minutes. Drain well off the tough brown skin and pat dry.

2 In a large pot, preheat oil to 375°F. Fry yucca in batches until golden brown on the outside. Drain on paper towel to absorb extra oil. Sprinkle with kosher salt. Serve immediately.

NOTE A woody core runs along the root's center. It should be removed or cut away when it's cut open.

Yucca (cassava) should be stored in the refrigerator for no more than 4 or 5 days after purchasing it.

Yield: 6 servings based on using 3 yuccas

SWEET POTATO LATKES

WITH FRENCH ONION DIP

The combination of sweet potatoes and white potatoes are a great variation on the traditional latke. I usually make both types and alternate them on a platter around a bowl of my famous French onion sour cream dip. Use chilled applesauce for a pareve dipping option.

Latkes:

3 sweet potatoes, peeled

3 Yukon or russet potatoes, peeled

6 eggs

1 scallion or green onion, chopped finely

1 Tbsp kosher salt

Freshly ground black pepper

Oil for frying

French Onion Dip:

2 Tbsp extra-virgin olive oil

1 extra-large Vidalia onion or 2 regular onions, sliced

2 cloves garlic, minced

1 Tbsp onion soup mix (without MSG) dissolved in ½ cup hot water

¼ tsp freshly ground black pepper

8 oz whipped cream cheese

2 cups sour cream (light works as well)

1 For latkes, grate potatoes finely and mix with remaining ingredients together in a large bowl.

2 Preheat a large frying pan with about half an inch of oil. Drop batter by table-spoonful into pan. Fry 3 to 4 minutes on each side, until brown and crispy. Remove from oil and drain on paper towels to absorb excess oil.

3 For French Onion Dip, heat olive oil in a large pot and add onions and garlic. Let cook on medium heat for 10 minutes until soft and slightly browned. Add dissolved onion soup mix and black pepper and let cook for 5 more minutes or until water has evaporated. Remove from heat and cool slightly.

4 Meanwhile, mix cream cheese and sour cream together in a large bowl. Add cooked onion mixture and combine very well. (I like to smooth out the texture with a few pulses from an immersion blender.) Refrigerate up to 3 days.

Yield: 12 servings

WARM BABY POTATOES

WITH CUMIN

When cumin is toasted in its whole form, it adds a warm and mellow flavor to the dish. You can use ground cumin in small amounts, but the flavor of home-toasted cumin is, in my opinion, much better.

2 lbs baby new potatoes

1 Tbsp whole cumin seeds

1 Tbsp mustard

1 ½ tsp honey

3 Tbsp olive oil

1 tsp fresh lemon juice

1 large scallion, finely chopped

Cook potatoes in a large pot of salted boiling water until they can be pierced easily with a fork (about 25 minutes). Drain well.

Meanwhile, place cumin seeds in a heavy skillet and place over medium heat. Toast the seeds, stirring occasionally, until some start to pop or the smell gets very strong. Remove and cool. Crush toasted cumin with a mortar and pestle, or place in a plastic bag and press with a rolling pin.

Combine mustard, honey, olive oil, and lemon juice in a large bowl. Add potatoes and toss gently to coat. Add scallions and sprinkle with crushed cumin, just a bit at a time, adjusting the seasoning to your taste. Toss again and serve.

Yield: 6 to 8 servings

TZIMMES

Tzimmes is traditionally eaten on Rosh Hashanah, as symbolism that our zechuyos (merits) should be numerous. The use of honey in this recipe makes it even more appropriate for that time of year.

3 Tbsp oil

½ Spanish onion, chopped

2 15-oz cans sliced carrots, well-drained

5 Tbsp honey

½ tsp kosher salt

Freshly ground black pepper

Juice of 1 large orange

¾ to 1 cup pitted prunes

¼ tsp ground cinnamon (optional)

1 Place a pan or shallow pot over medium heat and heat oil.

2 Sauté the onions until transparent. Add carrots, honey, salt, and pepper and mix. Cover pan and let cook over low heat for 20 minutes, gently mixing once or twice.

3 Add orange juice, prunes, and cinnamon (if using) and cover again. Let simmer on low for another 30 to 45 minutes or until juice gets absorbed. Mix occasionally to prevent carrots from sticking to the pan. Serve warm.

NOTE Cooking over a slow, steady fire is the trick to delicious tzimmes.

VARIATION You can add lemon zest before serving for a burst of flavor, or try substituting dried apricots for the prunes.

Yield: 8 servings

BROCCOLI SPINACH SOUFFLÉ

This light and tasty side dish goes well with both meat and fish. When making in advance and freezing, make sure the soufflés are well covered to avoid any freezer taste. To serve, simply thaw to room temperature and then bake, uncovered, at 350° F for about 15 minutes. This is one of those recipes that people constantly tell me they make often and enjoy.

1 lb broccoli stems and florets

1 lb spinach

¼ cup quick-cooking cream of wheat (farina)

1 cup boiling water

1 small onion

1 clove fresh garlic

4 eggs

2 heaping Tbsp light mayonnaise

1¼ tsp Kosher salt

1 tsp white pepper

½ tsp ground rosemary (optional)

Cornflake crumbs for topping

1 Preheat oven to 375°F.

2 Wash broccoli and spinach well and let dry completely. (If using frozen, place in a strainer and let defrost. All excess water should be squeezed out.) Meanwhile, place farina in a bowl and add boiling water. Cover with aluminum foil immediately and let stand for 10 minutes.

3 In a food processor fitted with the steel blade, pulse onions and garlic until fine. Add farina, broccoli and spinach; process until fine. In another bowl, place eggs, mayonnaise, salt, pepper, and rosemary (optional); mix well. Add broccoli and spinach mixture and stir until combined.

4 Spoon into greased muffin tins. Bake for 35 to 40 minutes.

Yield: 12 individual soufflés

HEIMISHE CARROT KUGELS

*Always a hit, carrot kugels
are delicious served warm
or at room temperature.
These are so simple to
make and can easily be
made in advance. Add half
a cup of chopped toasted
pecans to the batter to add
a bit of texture.*

2 eggs

½ cup oil or margarine

½ cup brown sugar (lightly packed)

½ cup sugar

1 cup flour

2 tsp baking powder

1 Tbsp vanilla sugar

1 Tbsp orange juice

2 cups very finely grated carrots

1 tsp ground cinnamon

1 Preheat oven to 350°F. Grease 10 compartments of a mufffin pan or a 9-inch round pan.

2 Place all the ingredients in a large mixing bowl and stir until combined.

3 Spoon into prepared pan.

4 Bake 45 minutes for muffins and 1 hour using a round pan, until nicely browned.

NOTE These kugels freeze very well.

Yield: 10 servings

ROASTED VEGETABLES

There is no special rule as to which vegetables to use when roasting. I have chosen the ones listed here simply because I like them. Be creative and try other vegetables as well! Roasting is my favorite cooking method when preparing vegetables.

1 lb thin carrots, peeled

1 lb parsnips, peeled and sliced

1 large bulb fennel

½ lb shallots

2 Tbsp extra-virgin olive oil

Sea salt or kosher salt

Freshly ground black pepper

2 Tbsp pure maple syrup

1 Preheat oven to 400°F.

2 Cut all vegetables into similar-sized pieces. Lay flat on a cookie sheet or roasting pan and drizzle with olive oil, salt, and pepper. Mix to coat all the vegetables evenly and spread them in a single layer.

3 Roast uncovered for 25 minutes, stirring once or twice. Add maple syrup and mix once again to coat evenly. Return to oven for an additional 5 to 7 minutes. Serve warm or at room temperature.

NOTE For maximum flavor, buy carrots with the green still attached. Cut off greens as close to the base as possible.

Yield: 8 servings

PEAS IN BREA CRUMBS

This combination may seem a bit unusual, but somehow, the flavors blend together and it works beautifully! This side dish is a great accompaniment for poultry and fish alike.

1 ½ cups fresh shelled peas (use frozen peas if fresh peas are unavailable)

1 ½ Tbsp olive oil

1 cup panko crumbs

½ tsp kosher salt

½ tsp freshly ground black pepper

1 tsp dried basil

1 tsp dried thyme

½ tsp garlic powder

½ tsp onion powder

1 ½ tsp fresh lemon zest

1　Bring a pot of salted water to a boil. Add peas, cover and cook about 3 to 5 minutes. The color of the peas will turn an even brighter green.

2　Transfer to a strainer and drain well, then rinse immediately with cold water to stop the cooking.

3　Preheat a thick saucepan or skillet on medium-high heat; add olive oil and heat slightly. Add crumbs along with all remaining ingredients except lemon zest. Cook crumb mixture in oil until light brown and toasted, about 5 minutes, stirring often to avoid burning.

4　Add peas, toss to coat and remove from heat to prevent overcooking.

5　Stir in lemon zest and serve immediately.

NOTE　Panko bread crumbs are often used in Japanese cooking. They are coarser than regular bread crumbs and have a delicious, crunchy taste.

Yield: 4 servings

EGGPLANT FRIES

WITH TAHINI DRESSING

This tasty, high-in-protein snack (or side dish) is great for a low-carb diet, and for anyone who appreciates Middle-Eastern flavors. You won't believe how good these are until you've tried them!

3 to 4 Asian eggplants

3 Tbsp extra-virgin olive oil

1 Tbsp kosher salt

½ Tbsp freshly ground black pepper

Tahini Dressing

1 cup prepared tahini

2 cloves garlic, freshly minced

1 Tbsp fresh lemon juice

1 to 2 Tbsp water or plain yogurt

1　Preheat oven to 350ºF. Line a baking sheet with foil or parchment paper.

2　Cut eggplants into quarters, and then cut each wedge in half. Place slices on the lined baking sheet and drizzle olive oil over eggplant. Toss to coat eggplant, then sprinkle with kosher salt and black pepper.

3　Bake uncovered for 40 minutes, tossing once during baking.

4　For Tahini Dressing, combine tahini, garlic, lemon juice and water or yogurt in a bowl and mix. Serve with Eggplant Fries.

NOTE　For a low-fat dairy version, try replacing the Tahini Dressing with low-fat yogurt.

Yield: 10 servings

MINI ORZO-STUFFED PEPPERS

2 cups dry orzo

2 Tbsp extra-virgin olive oil, divided use

2 cloves garlic, crushed

1 large zucchini, finely grated

1 (14 oz) can diced tomatoes (including juice)

1 Tbsp fresh basil, finely chopped (or 1½ tsp dried basil)

Kosher Salt

Freshly ground black pepper

10 mini peppers or 6 very small bell peppers

1 Cook the orzo in salted water according to package directions. When done, drain well. place in a large bowl and mix with 1 tablespoon olive oil. Set aside.

2 Meanwhile, sauté garlic in 1 tablespoon oil until fragrant (not brown). Add zucchini and diced tomatoes with juice. Cook until zucchini is soft, about 10 minutes. Then add basil, salt, and pepper. Pour vegetables into a strainer that is set over a bowl and reserve juices. Mix vegetables with cooked orzo.

3 Cut off the top of the peppers and cut out the ribs and seeds. Place in a deep greased baking dish (if using bell peppers, cut a tiny bit off the bottom to create a straight edge so that they can stand upright). Fill the peppers with the orzo mixture. Pour the reserved vegetable juice into the pan around the peppers. (Alternatively, you can use vegetable or chicken stock.)

4 Cover baking dish tightly and bake at 350°F for approximately 35 to 40 minutes. Serve warm or at room temperature..

Yield: 6 servings

BARBEQUE CORN

Grilled corn on the cob is a special summertime treat. This combination adds a unique flavor — something like barbeque flavored popcorn!

6 ears of corn

2 Tbsp olive oil

1 tsp Montreal steak spice or any steak spice

¾ tsp paprika

¾ tsp kosher salt

Freshly ground pepper

1 Soak the ears of corn, together with their husks, in a large bowl of cold water for about 20 minutes or up to 2 hours.

2 When ready to cook, preheat the grill to medium heat. Pull any extra exterior leaves off the corn but leave one layer. Gently fold that layer back and tear out the silky threads from within.

3 Combine all the ingredients listed above in a small bowl and rub mixture on the corn ears generously to coat them. Pull husks back up around corn and tie with a piece of loose husk or twine. Place on preheated grill and cook for about 20 to 30 minutes, turning occasionally to prevent charring.

4 Serve warm with melted butter or margarine if desired.

NOTE You will know corn is ready when you press a kernel and the juice shoots out.

Yield: 6 servings

GRILLED TOMATOES AND BALSAMIC DRESSING

Grilled tomatoes are especially tasty with grilled chicken quarters or chicken breasts. These tomatoes can be prepared two or three hours in advance, but pour dressing on right before serving.

4 large "beefsteak" tomatoes, sliced

1 Tbsp extra-virgin olive oil

Kosher salt or sea salt

Freshly ground black pepper

Dressing:

½ cup of fresh basil leaves, finely chopped

¼ cup extra-virgin olive oil

1 Tbsp balsamic vinegar

Kosher salt and freshly ground black pepper to taste

1   Preheat grill to high heat.

2   Brush tomato slices with olive oil, sprinkle with salt and pepper, and grill on each side for about 2 to 3 minutes or until slightly soft.

3   Mix ingredients for dressing in a small bowl.

4   Remove tomatoes from grill, place on a serving platter and pour dressing over. Can be served warm or chilled.

NOTE   If you don't have a grill, roast tomatoes uncovered at 400° F in the oven for about 6 to 8 minutes.

Beefsteak tomatoes are the largest variety of cultivated tomatoes and can weigh up to 1 lb each.

Yield: 8 servings

SUSHI PIZZA

This is a different and beautiful version of sushi that anyone can make. It's fast, easy, and beautiful. Choose any toppings you prefer for your pizza.

2 cups sushi rice

3 cups water

¹⁄₃ cup rice vinegar

2 Tbsp sugar

1 tsp table salt

Toppings options:

Mango

Small seedless cucumbers

Avocado (See Note)

Fresh salmon

Lox (3 to 4 oz)

1 Place the rice and water in a pot over high heat and bring to a boil. Reduce heat to low, cover the pot, and cook for 12 minutes. Remove pot from heat but leave covered for 10 minutes more.

2 Meanwhile, in a small bowl, mix the vinegar, sugar, and salt together until dissolved. Add to rice and mix for 5 minutes or until cool.

3 Line a 10-inch round springform pan with plastic wrap. Cut desired toppings into very thin slices or wedges and arrange in the bottom of the pan in an attractive design. Place rice on top and press gently to form a smooth layer. Cover again with plastic wrap and place another round pan (or the bottom of another springform pan) onto the rice and weigh it down with cans. Refrigerate for 1 hour or overnight.

4 Undo sides of springform pan and remove. Place a large round plate over rice and carefully flip the "pizza" over onto it. Remove plastic and slice pizza into wedges. Serve with wasabi or soy sauce.

NOTE I prepared the whole pizza in advance, but added the avocado just before serving to avoid browning.

Yield: 10 servings

BLACK OLIVE PÂTÉ AND WHITE BEAN PÂTÉ

Be adventurous and add a bit of Middle-Eastern flavor to your table. These two dips are so simple to make and will add a delicious new twist to any meal. Serve with hummus and toasted pita chips.

Black Olive Pâté:

1 19 oz can pitted black olives, drained

1 tsp lemon juice

1 garlic clove, crushed

1 Tbsp extra-virgin olive oil

½ tsp freshly ground black pepper

White Bean Pâté:

1 19 oz can white beans, drained

1 tsp lemon juice

1 garlic clove, crushed

1 Tbsp extra-virgin olive oil

½ tsp freshly ground black pepper

1 tsp parsley flakes

½ tsp kosher salt

Black Olive Pâté Rinse olives well. Place all ingredients in a bowl, and blend with an immersion blender until smooth.

White Bean Pâté Rinse white beans well. Place white beans, lemon juice, garlic, olive oil, and pepper in a bowl. Blend with an immersion blender until smooth. Add parsley flakes and salt and mix to combine.

Yield: Black Olive Pâté, 12 servings, White Bean Pâté, 6 servings

GREEN BEANS

WITH SESAME SEEDS

Toasted sesame oil takes everyday green beans up a level. It doesn't take more than a few minutes to prepare this beautiful and tasty side dish. I cut the beans into bite-size pieces to make it easier for little people to eat, but you can leave them whole if you prefer.

1 lb green beans

1 lb wax or yellow beans

1 Tbsp canola oil

2 tsp toasted sesame oil, divided use

Kosher or sea salt

Freshly ground black pepper

1½ tsp white sesame seeds

1 tsp black sesame seeds

1   Trim ends off beans and cut into bite-size pieces. Bring a pot of water to a boil. Add beans and cook just until the color brightens and the beans are just softening slightly – about 3 to 5 minutes. Drain immediately and run beans under cold water to stop the cooking. Drain well and pat dry with paper towels.

2   Heat canola oil in a wok or large frying pan. Add half the toasted sesame oil as well as the beans, and stir-fry on medium-high heat for 2 minutes, constantly moving them as they cook. Add the rest of the sesame oil, salt, and a generous amount of freshly ground black pepper. Toss to coat beans, and add sesame seeds. Stir and serve warm or at room temperature.

Yield 6 to 8 servings

LEEK SWIRLS

Leeks are one of the symbols of Rosh Hashanah. They are part of the onion family and have a milder flavor. These can be frozen raw and baked when needed.

6 to 8 leeks

3 Tbsp oil

Kosher salt and freshly ground black pepper

6 sheets mallawach dough (approximately) (See Note)

Dijon mustard for spreading

1 egg yolk for brushing

1   Preheat oven to 375°F. Line a baking sheet with parchment paper.

2   Remove the green parts and root ends from each leek. (Only the light-colored middle section should be used.) Wash each layer well and then place on a clean towel to dry for a few minutes. Chop up very fine.

3   Place oil into a large skillet and heat on medium heat. Add leeks and reduce heat to low. Sauté slowly for at least ½ hour, until leeks are soft and tender. Sprinkle with kosher salt and freshly ground black pepper. Let cool.

4   Remove a piece of dough from the package and roll it gently into a rectangle. Smear with a thin layer of Dijon mustard. Top with 2 heaping tablespoons of leeks and spread evenly.

5   Roll up, jelly-roll style. Cut into 1-inch pieces and place swirl-side up on a lined baking sheet. Brush with egg yolk.

6   Bake 25 to 30 minutes, just until golden. Best served immediately or reheat uncovered for a few minutes at serving time.

NOTE   Mallawach is a Yemenite dough that is similar to flaky dough but with a richer taste. It is sold in the freezer section of many large kosher supermarkets and is often imported from Israel. A popular brand is Soglowek Ltd. If you can't find it, use flaky dough or puff pastry instead.

Yield: approximately 42

GRILLED ASPARAGUS

WITH HOLLANDAISE DRESSING

Thyme adds a subtle flavor to the asparagus, making it a quick and tasty side dish. This dish is best when served fresh, so make the dressing earlier and get the asparagus ready. Then all you have to do is broil it close to serving time.

Hollandaise Dressing:

4 Tbsp light mayonnaise

1 Tbsp mustard

2 tsp fresh lemon juice

1 tsp fresh lemon zest

1 tsp dried thyme (or 1 Tbsp fresh thyme leaves, finely chopped)

Chopped fresh chives to garnish

1 lb asparagus

1 to 2 Tbsp extra-virgin olive oil

Kosher salt

Freshly ground black pepper

3 sprigs fresh thyme

1 To make the Hollandaise Dressing, mix together all ingredients in a bowl, cover and refrigerate until just before serving time.

2 Cut off both the top and bottom of each asparagus spear. Remove the small triangles at the top of each stalk with either a sharp knife or vegetable peeler to free the asparagus from any bugs that could potentially be hiding under them. Wash thoroughly and pat dry.

3 Arrange asparagus in a single layer on a greased baking pan and brush with oil. Sprinkle generously with kosher salt and freshly ground black pepper. Place thyme sprigs on top of asparagus.

4 Right before serving, preheat oven to broil. Broil asparagus about 4 inches away from heating element until tender and slightly browned, 8 to 10 minutes, shaking pan at half time to turn the spears.

5 Cool slightly, top with Hollandaise and serve.

NOTE The easiest way to clean asparagus is to simply peel it. With a light hand, remove only a thin layer of skin. This will create a tender texture and help the asparagus cook more evenly.

Yield: 4 servings

CRANBERRY SAUCE

Fresh cranberries are only available for a short amount of time each winter. When I find them fresh, I make this delicious sauce to accompany almost any meat or poultry. The recipe works well with frozen whole cranberries as well. You can make half the recipe for a small family.

24 oz fresh or frozen cranberries (2 bags)

1 cup orange juice

1 cup water

1¾ cups sugar

2 Tbsp cornstarch dissolved in ¼ cup cold water

1 Combine cranberries, orange juice, water and sugar in a large saucepan and mix well. Bring to a slow boil. Reduce heat and cook on medium heat, stirring occasionally, until skins of cranberries start to pop, about 10 minutes.

2 Add dissolved cornstarch mixture and cook a few more minutes until liquid begins to thicken, stirring occasionally.

3 Remove from heat and let cool completely. Transfer cranberry sauce to a covered container and refrigerate. Serve chilled with smoked turkey breast.

NOTE This keeps about a week in the refrigerator. Do not freeze.

Yield: about 4½ cups sauce

LOW-FAT VEGETABLE SOUFFLÉS

This recipe was originally developed for an Israeli company named Shibolim, manufacturers of high-quality whole grain products. The matzo ball mix adds wonderful flavor and is a great binding ingredient in these light vegetable kugels. They can also be made in two 8-inch round pans.

⅓ cup extra-virgin oil

1 clove garlic, minced

1 large Spanish onion, chopped

6 medium carrots, peeled and grated

3 medium zucchini, unpeeled and grated

1½ Tbsp kosher salt (or 1 Tbsp table salt)

3 eggs

1 Tbsp sugar

¼ tsp black pepper

1 package (4.5 oz) whole wheat matzo ball mix (see Note)

1 tsp dried basil

1 Preheat oven to 375°F. Spray compartments of a muffin pan generously with cooking spray.

2 Place oil, garlic, onions and grated carrots in a large, shallow pot. Let sauté slowly for about 20 minutes, stirring occasionally.

3 Meanwhile, set a strainer filled with the grated zucchini over a bowl to catch the liquid that drains out. Sprinkle with salt and let zucchini drain for 20 minutes. Discard liquid.

4 Place eggs, sugar, black pepper, matzo ball mix and dried basil in a large bowl. Add drained zucchini and cooled carrot mixture. Mix well.

5 Scoop into muffin tins, filling them to the top. Bake 45 to 50 minutes.

NOTE Instead of whole wheat matzo ball mix, you can substitute one package (4 oz/125 g) regular matzo ball mix, using both packets.

Yield: 1 dozen

WHOLE WHEAT ORZO

I originally developed this recipe for Shibolim of Israel, producers of a line of all-natural whole grain products. This wonderful combination of colors, along with a sophisticated blend of ingredients, enhances whole wheat orzo, which is rice-shaped pasta. This versatile side dish goes perfectly with meat or poultry. If you don't fancy the flavor of ginger, you can omit it with excellent results.

6 cups water

2 cups vegetable or chicken stock

1 Tbsp extra-virgin olive oil

½ tsp salt

1 pkg (9 oz) whole wheat orzo

2 Tbsp extra-virgin olive oil

1 Spanish onion, chopped

1 Tbsp freshly minced ginger (optional)

¼ cup dried cranberries

¼ cup toasted slivered almonds

¼ tsp freshly ground black pepper

2 Tbsp chopped fresh Italian parsley

1 tsp grated lemon zest

1   In a large saucepan, bring water, soup stock, 1 Tbsp olive oil and salt to a boil. Add orzo and bring to a second boil. Cook uncovered 12 to 14 minutes or until orzo is "al dente." Drain well.

2   Meanwhile, heat 2 Tbsp oil in a large skillet on medium heat. Add onion and sauté until transparent. Add ginger and sauté 1 to 2 minutes longer, until ginger becomes fragrant.

3   Add dried cranberries, almonds, and black pepper to skillet and mix gently.

4   Add cooked orzo and toss thoroughly.

5   Add chopped parsley and lemon zest just before serving. Delicious served warm or at room temperature.

Yield: 4 servings

TURNIP

RADISH

CELERY ROOT

CARROT

breads

soup

salads

fish

meat + poultry

sides

dairy
dishes

CRISPY POTATOES

WITH SHALLOTS AND DILL

While this may not be an unusual or dramatically different side dish, crispy potatoes are one of those foods you can never get tired of. Serve them as suggested below and they will be a real hit! I serve this to my kids as a dairy meal but it's also a wonderful side dish!

2 lbs mini red potatoes

2 Tbsp extra-virgin olive oil

2 Tbsp butter

1 tsp kosher salt

½ tsp freshly ground black pepper

1 to 2 shallots, finely shredded

2 Tbsp fresh dill, chopped

1 cup sour cream

Freshly ground black pepper

1 Cut the mini potatoes in half.

2 Melt oil and butter in a large non-stick skillet. Place potatoes cut side down in a single layer (try to fit as many as possible, the rest can just sit on top of them). Cover the pan and let cook on medium-low heat until potatoes are soft and outsides are crunchy – about half an hour. Check occasionally to see if bottom slices are getting too dark. If they are, add a little oil (about 1 tablespoon) and mix the potatoes so they all get crispy and brown. Sprinkle with salt and pepper.

3 To serve, top with shredded shallots and chopped fresh dill. Serve in a large serving dish with a generous dollop of sour cream and sprinkle with additional freshly ground black pepper.

Yield: 4 to 6 servings

ROASTED TOMATO SPAGHETTI
WITH RICOTTA

When I see those gorgeous heirloom tomatoes with their interesting shapes and vibrant colors, I often can't resist the urge to buy them and create something delicious. This recipe is a result of one of those occasions.

1 lb mixed heirloom tomatoes (or red and yellow grape tomatoes)

4 shallots, trimmed and cut in quarters

2 Tbsp olive oil

Kosher salt

Freshly ground black pepper

¼ cup additional olive oil

3 cloves garlic, minced

1 Tbsp dried basil

4 cups cooked spaghetti

1 cup ricotta cheese

1 Preheat oven to 400°F.

2 If tomatoes are large, cut them in halves or quarters. Mix tomatoes and shallots with 2 tablespoons olive oil and spread out on a large baking sheet. Sprinkle with salt and pepper. Roast uncovered for 15 minutes, until tender.

3 Meanwhile, heat ¼ cup olive oil in a pan. Remove from heat and add minced garlic and basil. Let cool.

4 Remove tomatoes and shallots from oven and place in a large mixing bowl. Pour olive oil mixture over and mix gently to coat.

5 While tomatoes are roasting, cook pasta according to package directions. Drain well. Let cool until lukewarm.

6 Mix pasta with ricotta cheese. Add roasted tomato mixture and mix.

NOTE For a low-fat version, try using 1% cottage cheese in place of ricotta.

You can keep this dish pareve by omitting the ricotta cheese.

The tomato mixture can be made up to 2 days in advance.

Yield: 4 servings

COTTAGE CHEESE PANCAKES

6 eggs

2 cups 2% cottage cheese

¼ cup sugar

⅔ cup flour

½ tsp baking powder

¼ tsp kosher salt

¼ tsp ground cinnamon

½ cup raisins (optional)

Oil for frying

1   Place eggs in a bowl and whisk well until foamy (or use an immersion blender to create the volume). Combine all remaining ingredients in another mixing bowl and mix well.

2   Pour half of foamy egg mixture into cottage cheese mixture and fold gently until combined, using a rubber spatula. Slowly add the mixture back into the other half of the foamy egg mixture and once again, fold together gently to combine.

3   Place 1 tablespoon of oil in a frying pan and heat on medium heat. Pour half a ladleful of batter for each pancake into the pan.

4   Cook 2 to 3 minutes per side, until golden brown. Repeat with remaining batter, adding oil as necessary to the pan.

NOTE You can refrigerate the batter overnight, but the mixture will lose its volume. They still taste great, though!

Yield: 8 servings

DEEP-DISH PARTY PIZZA SQUARES

Pizza is everybody's favorite party food — whatever the age. Treat your guests or family to this homemade deep-dish version, which is sure to be a great hit. The dough can be made the day before and refrigerated. Before using, make sure the dough comes to room temperature and then rises for 20 minutes more.

Dough:

2⅓ cups warm water

2 tsp active dry yeast or ¾ oz fresh yeast

2 tsp sugar

6 cups all-purpose flour

3 Tbsp olive oil

2 tsp salt

Topping:

Canola or peanut oil for frying

2 cups button mushrooms

4 to 5 shallots, sliced thinly

2 cups pizza sauce (approximately)

4 to 5 cups grated pizza cheese blend

1　In a large bowl of an electric mixer fitted with a dough hook, combine water, yeast and sugar until it proofs or bubbles, about 5 minutes. Add the flour, olive oil, and salt last and mix well for about 3 to 4 minutes. Cover with a kitchen towel and let rest for about half an hour in a warm area.

2　Meanwhile, preheat a small, deep pot filled with 2 inches of canola or peanut oil to approximately 350°F. Add button mushrooms (cut to desired size) and shallots. It will take less than a minute for them to fry. Remove with a slotted spoon and drain on paper towel to absorb excess oil.

3　Preheat oven to 400°F.

4　Once dough has risen, rub your palms with olive oil and press dough into a rimmed, greased pan about 13 inches by 21 inches, or 2 roasting pans. Smooth dough out so that it reaches the corners of the pan. Smear dough evenly with pizza sauce and sprinkle liberally with pizza cheese.

5　Bake in preheated oven for 22 to 25 minutes. Cut into desired-size pieces and sprinkle generously with mushrooms and shallots. Serve immediately.

Yield: 12 servings

CHEESY SPRING ROLLS

WITH MARINARA SAUCE

24 spring roll wrappers

24 individual string cheeses, unwrapped

Canola or peanut oil for deep-frying

Marinara Sauce:

1 small onion, finely diced

1 to 2 cloves garlic, minced

3 Tbsp olive oil

1 can (28 oz) diced or whole tomatoes, undrained

1 can (6 oz) tomato paste

2 Tbsp sugar

½ tsp salt

1 bay leaf

1   Place a spring roll wrapper on the work surface with a corner pointed towards you. Place string cheese toward the bottom. Fold bottom corner over cheese, rolling once, and then fold in each side. Continue to roll up and wet the top corner with a wet pastry brush (or your fingers) so that the wrapper will stay closed. Press tightly to seal. Repeat with remaining wrappers and cheese.

2   For the Marinara Sauce, sauté onion and garlic in oil in a large saucepan or pot until soft. Add remaining ingredients and bring to a boil. Reduce heat and let simmer uncovered for 20 to 30 minutes or until thickened. Remove bay leaf.

3   In a deep pan or pot, heat oil to 375°F and fry cheese sticks in batches until brown, about 1 minute. Remove with slotted spoon and drain well on paper towels.. Serve with Marinara Sauce.

NOTE   Add spring rolls carefully to the hot oil to prevent splatters. Don't overcrowd the pan as this will bring down the temperature of the oil.

Yield: 24

CREAMY
PASTA
ROLLUPS

12 lasagne noodles

1 jar (about 3 cups) of your favorite marinara sauce

Filling:

500 g (about 1 lb) ricotta cheese

250 g (about ½ lb) cottage cheese (1% is fine)

1 cup shredded mozzarella or Cheddar cheese

2 eggs

½ tsp salt

½ tsp black pepper

¼ cup fresh Italian parsley, chopped

1 or 2 scallions, finely chopped

½ cup toasted pine nuts

Preheat oven to 375°F.

Cook the lasagne noodles according to package directions, until al dente — soft but still chewy — and drain. Lay noodles flat.

Combine filling ingredients in a large bowl and mix thoroughly until smooth.

Grease a 9-inch square deep baking dish. Place approximately 2 heaping table-spoons of filling on the center of a lasagne noodle and spread evenly it to cover the whole noodle. Roll the noodle up gently and place seam down into the baking dish.

Repeat with the rest of the noodles, packing them in close together in the baking dish. Pour marinara sauce over the top of the noodles, covering them completely.

Cover the pan and bake for 40 minutes. Serve warm.

Yield: 4 servings

LOW-FAT PENNE A LA VODKA

This popular pasta dish is everybody's favorite. Aside from the fact that, where I live, dairy cream is only available at select times of the year, the fat content in most traditional recipes made me come up with this lower-fat version.

1 pkg (16 oz) penne

1 Tbsp extra-virgin olive oil

2 Tbsp butter

1 small onion, finely chopped

1 clove crushed garlic

1 tsp dried basil

½ tsp dried oregano

1 cup pizza sauce

1 tsp kosher salt (or less)

Freshly ground black pepper

3 cups low-fat milk (1% or 2%)

⅔ cup flour

2 bay leaves

1 Tbsp vodka

1 Cook noodles according to package directions. Drain well and set aside.

2 In a pan, combine olive oil and butter and melt over medium-low heat. Add onions and garlic; sauté slowly. After about 5 minutes, add basil and oregano along with pizza sauce, salt, and pepper. Let simmer on low heat until onions are soft — about 10 minutes.

3 Meanwhile, in another pan or pot, combine milk and flour and whisk until smooth. Add bay leaves and simmer on very low heat for 10 minutes, stirring occasionally. Remove bay leaves.

4 Mix the two sauces together until well combined. Stir in vodka, and toss with hot pasta. Serve immediately.

NOTE If your sauce is lumpy, you can use an immersion blender to smooth it out. To reheat the noodles, place in pot and add ⅓ cup milk, stir until all is combined, and warm again.

Yield: 4 o 6 servings

ZUCCHINI STICKS

WITH CHEESE AND BREAD CRUMBS

Here is a very tasty way to use up any extra bread crumbs or croutons you probably have sitting in your pantry. I have a feeling you'll be buying bread crumbs with this recipe in mind.

3 large zucchini (do not peel)

1 to 2 Tbsp extra-virgin olive oil

Kosher salt and freshly ground black pepper

1 cup flavored bread crumbs, panko crumbs, or leftover salad croutons, crushed

2 Tbsp extra-virgin olive oil or melted butter

1½ cups shredded Cheddar cheese

1 Preheat oven to 400°F.

2 Cut zucchini in half lengthwise and then in half again. Cut each wedge into 3-inch sticks. Place in an oven-safe baking dish; coat zucchini with olive oil and sprinkle with kosher salt and freshly ground black pepper. Cover and bake for 25 minutes.

3 Meanwhile, place the bread crumbs in a bowl and mix with olive oil or melted butter.

4 Remove zucchini from oven when done. Sprinkle with cheese and then bread crumb mixture. Sprinkle some additional kosher salt and bake uncovered for 8 minutes. Serve hot.

VARIATION Brush zucchini with minced garlic before covering with cheese and bread crumb mixture.

NOTE When I make it, I like to use all three! The garlic salad croutons added great flavor. If you don't use flavored bread crumbs, add 1 tablespoon dried basil.

Yield: 6 servings

Crêpes:
6 Tbsp flour
5 Tbsp sugar
5 eggs
1 cup milk or club soda
1 Tbsp oil

Cheese filling:
8 oz feta cheese
12 oz ricotta cheese

Spinach mixture:
16 oz bag frozen spinach
2 cloves garlic, minced
1 Tbsp olive oil
½ tsp freshly ground black pepper
Less than 1 tsp kosher salt

Store-bought salsa, for serving

Whisk together crêpe ingredients in a large bowl until smooth.

Grease a non-stick pan. Using a ladle, pour enough batter into the pan to coat the bottom evenly. (You may have to swirl the pan in a circular motion to create an even layer of batter.) Once the batter solidifies into a crêpe (about 1 minute), turn it over and cook on the other side for 30 seconds. Remove from pan.

To make cheese filling, mix feta cheese and ricotta cheese in a bowl to combine.

To make spinach mixture, place frozen spinach in a strainer to defrost. Press firmly on spinach to remove excess water. Sauté the garlic in a large skillet in olive oil until fragrant (not brown). Add spinach and sauté about 5 minutes or until extra water has disappeared. Add salt and pepper.

To assemble crêpes, place about 2 to 3 tablespoons of cheese mixture into the center of each crêpe and 1 to 2 tablespoons of spinach filling on top. Roll up and cover until ready to serve.

Gently heat the salsa in a small pan or in the microwave. Pour over warm crêpes before serving.

There is no need to grease the pan between each crêpe – after every 4 or 5 crêpes is sufficient.

Yield: approximately 10 to 12 crêpes

RUSTIC TOMATO TART

You can make these tarts as individual servings or in 2 8-inch round pans (preferably with removable bottoms); they can be served warm or at room temperature.

Dough:

1 cup flour

½ cup (1 stick) butter

2 egg yolks

½ tsp kosher salt

3 Tbsp ice water

Topping:

20 oz fresh mozzarella

10 to 12 tomatoes in assorted colors

20 basil leaves (approximately)

4 Tbsp olive oil

4 cloves garlic, minced

Kosher salt and freshly ground black pepper

1. Pulse flour, butter, egg yolks, and salt in a food processor fitted with a steel blade. Add ice water and pulse just until dough comes together. Do not overprocess.

2. Remove dough from machine. Knead a few times between your fingers and form into a disc shape. Cover well with plastic wrap and refrigerate for 1 hour or overnight.

3. Preheat the oven to 375°F. Remove pastry dough from the fridge and allow about 10 minutes to get it to room temperature.

4. Divide dough into 2 pieces and roll each piece on a lightly floured surface into an 8-inch round. Press each dough circle into the bottom of an ungreased 8-inch pan. Prick all over with a fork and bake in the oven for about 10 minutes.

5. Allow pastry to cool slightly, and reduce oven temperature to 350°F.

6. Slice the mozzarella cheese thinly and arrange slices over the pastry base. Top with a single layer of sliced tomatoes, letting them overlap slightly.

7. Dip basil leaves in olive oil and arrange them on top of the tomatoes. Brush tomatoes and basil with minced garlic and leftover olive oil. Sprinkle with salt and pepper.

8. Bake for 40 to 45 minutes. Serve warm.

NOTE I use the fresh mozzarella marinated in spices, made by Ko-sure, available in a vacuum-packed package. You can use plain mozzarella if you prefer, but the spicy one adds great flavor.

TIP If you're cooking for a smaller crowd, make one tart (using half the topping ingredients) and freeze half the dough.

Yield: 10 to 12 servings

GLOSSARY

Challah – traditional loaf of bread for Shabbat and Yom Tov, often braided

Charoset – a traditional mixture of apples, wine, walnuts used at the Passover seder

Pesach – the holiday of Passover

Purim – a Jewish holiday that takes place in March

Rosh Hashanah – the first day of the Jewish calendar

Seder – the traditional meal of the first nights of Passover

Shabbos – Sabbath – the seventh day of the week

Shalosh Seudos - also called Seudat Shelishis – the third meal of shabbot, eaten late Saturday afternoon

Tsimmis – a combination of carrots and honey usually eaten on Rosh Hashanah

Yom Tov – a Jewish holiday

INDEX

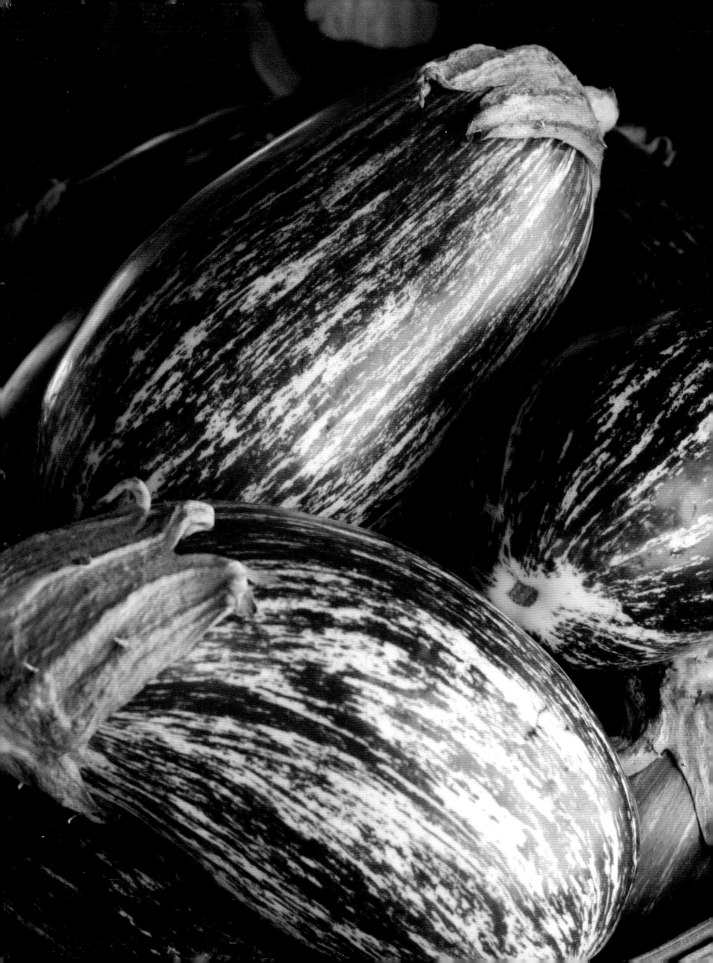